Edited by Mary-Lou Jennings

HUMPHREY JENNINGS
Film-Maker/Painter/Poet

British Film Institute in association with Riverside Studios
1982

Publisher's Note

2 This book aims to illustrate the many facets of Humphrey Jennings's career —
as film-maker, as photographer, as painter and as writer. It has been produced in
conjunction with the Jennings exhibition at Riverside Studios in London in
January/February 1982, supported by the Elephant Trust. Publication of this book
to accompany the exhibition was made possible with the aid of a grant to Riverside
Studios from the Arts Council of Great Britain.

   The book has, however, been produced with other readers in mind
besides those visiting the exhibition, and the materials assembled here are intended
to be able to stand on their own as a guide to the diversity, and at the same time the
extraordinary coherence, of a unique body of artistic work. The book presents a lot
of new and original material, but in a way that is intended to be suggestive, not
definitive. We hope that, in conjunction with the exhibition, it will act as a stimulus
to a long overdue revaluation and reinterpretation of Jennings's work.

Films

Jennings's films were almost all produced for sponsors. Up to 1940 he worked
mainly for the GPO Film Unit, which was put under the auspices of the Ministry of
Information early in the war and became the Crown Film Unit in 1941. The MOI
was disbanded in 1946 and its surviving functions passed to the Central Office of
Information. Crown's producer during the war, Ian Dalrymple, left to form his own
company, Wessex Films, and in the post-war period Jennings worked on films for
Wessex as well as for Crown, but the COI remained the sponsor. Copyright on the
pre-war films resides with the Post Office, and on the wartime and post-war films
with the COI, but distribution prints of most of the major films are available from
the BFI. The Post Office and the Imperial War Museum also hold some distribution
prints. 35mm viewing copies are held in the National Film Archive and Imperial
War Museum collections. Many of the film stills in this book are taken direct from
the frame; the remainder are production stills. When production stills have been
used to illustrate the content of a film, this is indicated on the caption.

   Throughout the text the titles of films directed or co-directed by
Humphrey Jennings have been given in bold type: films by other directors (as well
as book titles, etc.) are in italic.

Paintings, Drawings, Photographs and Collages

Few of Humphrey Jennings's paintings and drawings are in public collections.
Those illustrated here are in the vast majority drawn from the private collection of
Charlotte Jennings (Jennings & Daly collection) or from that of Mary-Lou Jennings:
these are captioned JD (with number) and MLJ respectively. Pictures from other
collections are captioned with the full name of the source. Only a few of Humphrey
Jennings's paintings and drawings are signed, dated or titled by the artist.
In such cases the caption gives the title in italics and the date without brackets.
In all other cases descriptive titles are given (in roman type), with any conjectural
information, such as dates, added in square brackets [. . .]. With rare exceptions,
photographs and collages cannot be dated with any exactitude, but all (except for
travel pictures) are probably within the years 1934-39. Only dates that are
reasonably exact and certain have been supplied.

Special thanks are due to Charlotte Jennings for her help in dating and
identifying pictures, and her co-operation in making so many of them available for
reproduction; and to David Mellor for further advice.

Acknowledgments

Text permissions: the authors and Institute of Contemporary Arts for reprint of
'A Note on Images' by Charles Madge and 'Humphrey Jennings' by Kathleen
Raine (1951); Lindsay Anderson and *Sight and Sound*, for 'Only Connect' (1954);
Times Newspapers Ltd, for reprint of review by Humphrey Jennings in the *Times
Literary Supplement*, 7 August 1948; the Humphrey Jennings estate for writings by
Humphrey Jennings: this arrangement copyright © British Film Institute 1982.

Picture permissions and credits: stills from the National Film Archive
and Mary-Lou Jennings; thanks to the Imperial War Museum for the loan of a print
of **Words for Battle** (Crown Copyright / COI) and to the National Film Archive for
Spare Time (Copyright the Post Office), **Listen to Britain** and **Diary for
Timothy** (Crown Copyright / COI); framestills by Jane Heywood and Roger Holman,
enlargements by Geoff Goode Photographics; paintings and drawings photographed
by Ray Abbott.

The editor and publisher would also like to thank: Julie Lawson, Jenny
Stein, Elaine Burrows, Teddy Carrick, Ian Dalrymple, Nora Dawson and
Rachel Low.

Editorial co-ordination by Geoffrey Nowell-Smith
Book designed by Richard Hollis

Foreword

It is now more than thirty-one years since Humphrey Jennings died after a fall on the rocks while exploring the coast of Poros for a new film and it is more than thirty years since the ICA organised the first major exhibition of his work. It is difficult to explain the lapse of time that has occured before a second exhibition should take place showing his paintings and other aspects of his activities which include photographs, drawings, collages, films, poems and his unfinished work *Pandaemonium*. Indeed the republication of the appreciations written for the ICA catalogue by his friends Charles Madge and Kathleen Raine make it clear that a genius of remarkable quality has been monstrously neglected, and Lindsay Anderson reaffirms this in his expert critique of Humphrey as 'the only real poet of the British cinema'.

I met Humphrey first in 1935 when with other enthusiasts we were planning the Surrealist exhibition that took place in London the following year. I was at once captivated by his unusual brilliance, the originality of his thought, his passion for exploration of the more obscure aspects of the arts, his erudition and his intuitive love of his native country. Later as I became aware of his work on his film **Fires Were Started** during the most harrowing days and nights of the blitz I greatly admired his cool and indomitable courage. I can only add my testimony that the assessment of his contribution to human thought and the appreciation of the complex fascination of his character is in no way exaggerated by his friends. They give authoritative accounts of the 'imaginative truth' that pervades every branch of Humphrey's work.

I am convinced of the urgency there is to bring to light again the subtle materialisations of his imagination and the perfection of his style.

Roland Penrose

Chronology and Documents
Compiled by Mary-Lou Jennings

Humphrey Jennings on Suffolk
beach / c.1948

Note on Presentation

In making this selection from my father's papers, I have tried first to give some idea of where he was and on what he was working throughout his life. Secondly, I have attempted to link up ideas and images which have appeared and reappeared in his work. Thirdly, I have brought together material which, as much as possible, reflects his thoughts and concerns during the production of a particular piece of work.

Essays on my father's life and work over the past thirty years have been based on memories of colleagues and friends which, valuable though they are (and that is why some of them have been republished here), nevertheless were written often with little knowledge of what my father himself was thinking about his work and in some cases there were factual inaccuracies. Again and again friends have said that it has been impossible for them to convey his presence and ideas because what marked him out was the way in which he conveyed them, talking and arguing vigorously with those around him. One feature of this selection is that it begins to show the energy with which his thoughts were conveyed.

I have divided his life up into five sections which deal first with childhood and his education in Cambridge; then Paris and painting; the GPO Film Unit, surrealism and Mass Observation; the war and the war-time films; and post-war work up to his death in 1950. I have selected from letters and from work in progress from film scripts and treatments and notebooks and poetry as I think that they show the development of his ideas between 1930 and 1950. Admirers of his films will find it helpful to look also at his paintings and read his poetry. Last, the letters between 1940 and 1944 in particular are important as reports on Britain at war.

I have made minimal spelling corrections and marked gaps in the excerpts [. . .].

Mary-Lou Jennings / Hammersmith, 1981

1907. Frank Humphrey Sinkler Jennings was born on 19 August 1907 at The Gazebo, Walberswick, Suffolk. His parents were Frank Jennings and Mildred Jessie Hall. Frank Jennings was an architect and born in Newmarket, Suffolk in 1877, the youngest of fourteen children. His father, Thomas Jennings, trained racehorses, notably *Gladiateur*, known as the Avenger of Waterloo, the first French horse to win the Derby, in 1865. Mildred Jessie Hall was the daughter of a solicitor and born in Lewisham, London in 1881. She was a talented painter and later ran a shop, first at Walberswick and later in Holland Street, London, selling imported French pottery and textiles.

With his parents / 1908

Childhood

When I was a child, there was a curious relation of horses and trains at Newmarket like this: My grandmother had a house up the Bury Road on the way to the heath. If you slept in the front of the house you were woken up in the morning by the sound of strings' hooves going out to exercise and then again, as they came back. Running along the bottom of the garden behind the house was a railway cutting and on the left was a tunnel mouth where the trains came out of Warren Hill. On the far side of the line there were long deserted platforms — Warren Hill Station; only used on race days. Out of the mouth of the tunnel there was a permanent lock of black smoke twisting upwards.

Beyond the Life of Man / unpublished n.d.

[Blythburgh] Church with plough / [c.1949] / JD44

Blythburgh 1910

It was a time of artists and bicycles and blue and white spotty dresses.
They had a little boy who was carried in the basket of his mother's bicycle and they used to picnic on the common between Walberswick and Blythburgh.
In the summer the gorse on the Common bright yellow and a spark from the train as it passed would set the dry bushes on fire.
How hot those flames of gorse, how hot even the day itself!
How cool the inside of Blythburgh Church — the shade of a great barn, from whose rafters and king-posts the staring angels outspread wooden wings.
The solemnity of a child.
The intensity of the sea-bird.

1943

6

1916-1926. Jennings went to the Perse School, Cambridge at that time under the headmastership of the redoubtable Dr W.H.Rouse. The Perse was noted for its progressive teaching of English and drama, classics and modern languages. Jennings took part in and designed scenery for a large number of plays while at the Perse and later while an undergraduate at Pembroke College.

Blythburgh Church / photo by H.J.

War and Childhood

I remember as a child by the ferry watching the soldiers testing horses for France. Farm-horses — chasing them naked down to the river while the men on the banks hallooed and shot off guns in the air. I remember the Scots fisher girls on Blackshore gutting the herring and singing in Gaelic. Scaly hands running in fish-blood, the last vessel dropping her sail at the pier's end, the last fish kicking the net. But today there is nothing — nothing of the girls or the boats or the nets or the songs or even the fishmarket itself. Utterly gone — only the wind and broken glass and rough tiles made smooth by the sea. Only still visions of bloodshot eyes brimming over with fear.

1943

7

To Walberswick

All the memorials of this part of the world, as far back as the written word stretches, are reports of disaster — fire, flood, encroachments of the sea, poverty, oppression, decline, war and the military, destruction of common rights.

To the east is the sea. The sea-coast consist of sand-dunes, shingle, clayey cliffs, which are continually eaten away by the waves at their base and so slide into the main. Then the winds and the tides will silt up the river's mouth or break down the dykes and inundate the marshes and meadows and farmsteads far inland with winters of great flood. Then storms at sea will cast vessels on the banks of the Ness and batter them to pieces. Then fire will catch the dry grass on the common and spread from roof to roof. Then the townsfolk will come out on the marsh with billhooks and flails and defend the commons against the Lord's men.

Unwritten the story of the people's resistance, uncelebrated in word their struggle and labour. But the church towers from the past, the jetties and piers, the mills and lighthouses, the farms and cottages, the roads and the ridiculous railway — in whatever state they may be now — we must never forget that they were made and built and created and tended by the people — not by those powers for whom they were put up or whose names they bear or whose money allowed them to call them theirs — into the actual making they had little or no part — it was the people and the people alone who had the knowledge and strength and skill and love to fit the sails in the windmill, the thatch to the barn, the wings to the wooden angels, the flashing reflector to the lighthouse lamp.

The range of the sea goes so many miles inland. [. . .]

1943

Cambridge

As we descended westward we saw the fen country covered with pity: the water darkened with fish, the air screaming — the most brilliant prismatic colours imaginable.

1941

King David

'King David' is beginning, as they say, to take shape — that means that we have made long lists of scenes, scenery, colours for lights and costumes, entries and exits etcetera. Now I am sorting old dresses and rolls of unused stuffs from past shows. This goes on in cold draughty 'rooms' in John's: everything deep in dust — no fire. Nothing looks so tawdry as dresses off the stage. Mrs Rootham shouts how many of each there are and what colours: I with trembling fingers write on the back of an envelope odd remarks like '2 doz Chinese pyjamas' or 'six fishermen's jumpers in odd blues'. Then with some of these under my arms, wrapped up to the neck I trail across cobbled courts slippery with ice — the drift snow blowing playfully round corners — and back to the warmth of home.

      Here one sits up till 2 a.m. doing tentative sketches of odd characters in pencil with dabs of poster colour and inks. Some of these look possible and are taken next morning to Dennis Arundell who is usually in bed in a purple dressing gown, with a typewriter on his bedspread & clouds of cigarette smoke. He is giving lists of lights to somebody: and gives vague criticisms — with an occasional 'Yes I like that one' — to the drawings which are finally taken back to Mrs Rootham & the dress-makers begin. But that stage is not due till March.

Letter to Cicely Cooper / 15 February 1929

At the present moment I have something like fifty costumes to design — among other things — in the next ten days or so: it is this film coming on top of 'King David', a film of the Civil War 1642 with fights on the backstairs of farmhouses, inns burnt down and escapes from haylofts: incidentally, how *does* one give an estimate for an inn kitchen to be burnt in the film-studio? that is the sort of thing I find myself suddenly asked.

Letter to Cicely Cooper / 27 February 1929

Costume design for *King David* / JD9

1926. He won a scholarship to Pembroke College, Cambridge to read English, where his tutor was Aubrey Attwater, friend of Robert Graves during the 1914-1918 War. In March he designed the scenery and costumes for a production of Thomas Heywood's *The Fair Maid of Perth* for the Marlowe Society. He also designed sets for the Amateur Dramatic Club's Christmas revue and took part in sketches.

1927. Jennings gained a First Class in Part I of the English Tripos and the Parkin Scholarship at Pembroke. He acted in a Cambridge Amateur Dramatic Club production of *At the Same Time* by A.P.Herbert. In December he designed the sets for a production at the Perse School and played a small part and he designed scenery for Dennis Arundell's production of Henry Purcell's *King Arthur* with enormous success.

1928. Jennings designed *The Soldier's Tale* by Stravinsky for its first public performance in Britain with Lydia Lopokova and Michael Redgrave, produced by Dennis Arundell and conducted by Boris Ord.

1929. In May he designed the scenery and costumes for a production of Honegger's *King David* produced by the Cambridge University Musical Society — its first production as a dramatic pageant in Britain. In June he gained Double First Honours in the English Tripos with a mark of Distinction in Part II. During this year he also designed costumes and scenery for the London Opera Festival productions of *Cupid and Psyche* and *Dido and Aeneas*. Some time early in the year he met Cicely Cooper, the sister of Edward Cooper, a younger contemporary of his at the Perse.

Cicely Cooper was born in 1908, the daughter of Richard Synge Cooper, a civil engineer who at his retirement was engineer for New Works for the London Midland and Scottish Railway at Euston. Both her parents were Anglo-Irish and she and her brothers were widely read and gifted in languages. In October he and Cicely Cooper married at Kensington Register Office. By then, Jennings had gained a bursary from the Goldsmiths Company for postgraduate research, in addition to the Foundress Scholarship from Pembroke, and began work on Thomas Gray.

1930. In March, Jennings designed the sets and costumes for *The Bacchae* of Euripides produced by J.T.Sheppard. He edited *Venus and Adonis* from the Quarto of 1593 for the Experiment Press and acted Bottom in a production of Purcell's *The Fairy Queen* which was produced by Dennis Arundell in early 1931.

H.J. / c.1933

Marlowe and Painting

You may remember Kathleen Raine and Hugh [Sykes Davies] were talking one night about Marlowe's 'Dido Queen of Carthage': I have been working on Marlowe the last month or so and especially on Dido with the result that I want to produce it sometime. This I talked to Hugh about [. . .] and also questioned Robert Eddison about the ADC stage. The position is this: it is a rollicking play with a relatively small cast, which can and should be played in front of a decor *simultané* (very cheap this). As I am a member of the ADC I can produce a show there for a much reduced rent and borrow their scenery lights etc. The casting is pretty easy. Now what better than this as an *Experiment* contribution to the Centenaire de Romantisme? There is no doubt that put on in the first half of next term for three performances and really well advertised by Gerald [Noxon] with *Experiment* names on the posters (John Davenport to play the heavy lover) — production and decor (if I may) by H.J. with [J.M.] Keynes and Manny [Forbes] and [George] Rylands really interested — we should more than pay expenses . . . Go and see the Delacroix exhibition at the Louvre . . . Keep your eye on works by Cossio, Ghika, Borès, Vines.

Letter to Julian Trevelyan / 20 July 1930

1931. Until May, Jennings worked on his Gray thesis but lack of money made him take a temporary teaching post at Bishop Wordsworth's School, Salisbury, whose headmaster was a former teacher at the Perse, F.C.Happold. This job ended in July and in August he went to Paris to work on designs for Cresta Silks. He returned in September and in October moved to 19a British Grove, Hammersmith, London.

1932. Jennings seems to have been working on research work and painting, based in Cambridge. In May he went to Paris and travelled to the south of France. He and his wife stayed with Gerald and Betty Noxon in Provence for some months late in that year.
At some point in late 1932 or early 1933 he and Cicely Jennings moved into 7 Round Church Street, Cambridge.

1933. Throughout 1933, Jennings worked at the Festival Theatre, Cambridge, painting and moving scenery. His eldest daughter was born in September and in the autumn they moved to 28 Bateman Street, Cambridge. He got testimonials from both Aubrey Attwater and I.A.Richards during June, perhaps in an attempt to get an academic job, but without success.

Degas

I am now writing in the Orangerie having walked round the exhibition one or two turns. Evidently Degas is very different to our conception derived from the usual pastels. His sculpture is here again: superb again I think it, and the pictures are almost entirely of one class: oils (no pastels) and oils by Degas with his eye on Ingres. You know the two great Ingres in London: M de Nowins at the NG and the head of an officer tucked away at the Tate: Nearly all the Degas here have something looking back to that side (portraitiste) of Ingres esp Degas' self portraits. Treatment of staring or dreaming eyes especially, then the same eyes are given to his sitters and to washerwomen and tramps. And in these pictures the paint has a parallel quality of thick contemplativeness Ingres-like finish and luminosity: Degas' staring and dreaming *at* the picture. No cleverness, no shimmer of ballet dresses — but thought — great thought. And in the colour too: black grey-blues indian reds: saturated colours. [. . .] The sculpture I still feel to be different and greater: because more direct: almost Indian in the rhythms of dancers, with no pastel to weaken the outline or colour to fidget.
Letter to Cicely Jennings / 17 August 1931 / Paris

I write to enquire whether you know anything about cheap villas, Chambres meublées or such like in Provence (St Trpoez — damn — or near it) for the summer. Terribly cheap essential. Do you know anyone who owns one or anything like that. How long are you going to be in Paris? I sit about and paint and try not to lose my temper with this country and its ludicrous inhabitants. [. . .] Very thrilled with Braque's new work and a new drawing by Roux reproduced in *Cahiers* [*d'Art*].
Letter to Julian Trevelyan / 22 April 1933 / London

The Marx Bros

I saw James [Reeves] yesterday and we went to the latest Marx Bros. film which I had to admit was terribly funny: surrealism for the million. Also to an excellent short at the Tatler with LL [Len Lye] and Jane, on Voodoo dances in West Africa.
Letter to Cicely Jennings / n.d. (1934)

1934. By June he had moved from Cambridge, although in the early part of the year he sent material from his work in progress on Thomas Gray to T.S.Eliot at the *Criterion*. There is no record of when he started work with the GPO Film Unit, but it can be assumed that it was by the middle of 1934. By the end of the year he had edited *The Story of the Wheel*, and directed **Post Haste**, produced by John Grierson, designed sets for *Pett and Pott*, directed by Alberto Cavalcanti, and himself directed **Locomotives**. He also played the part of an heroic telegraph boy in *The Glorious Sixth of June*, directed by Cavalcanti. By the autumn he and his family were at 6 Brandrum Road, Blackheath, near to the GPO studios.

Alberto Cavalcanti

Painters

How is 'the world of the picture dealers'? And if I ever collected enough bearable pictures do you know anyone who would take them? And so on. How is Hayter [S.W.Hayter] he does not seem to have had his Exhibition here. I am sorry I can't send you a photo of anything of mine: they are rather more like something now. In such time as I get to paint, I have been painting scenery — not designing simply painting — at the Festival [Theatre], which is however closing at the end of next term. Not enough to live on but something. The University is ahem going Marxist and *Life and Letters* has got to Jouhandeau and England is busy persuading itself for the seven millionth time that it is beginning to face reality. We are rather snugly situated here, and managing to let existing slide off our duck's back. But of course there is always the rent to pay. [. . .] The Auden's and Day Lewis's and so on are a positive menace. Bill [Empson] is well out of it in Japan. And after Roux? Anybody? Any poets? Hugnet and Hugnet and H. And then? Giacometti not too bad.

Letter to Julian Trevelyan / 15 March 1933

The GPO Film Unit

I don't know where to begin. The job, to begin with, is perfectly real — I have already begun work. [. . .] The hours are approximately 10 to 6 — or more like 10.30-6.30 — Half day Saturday: Sunday off. They are taking me seriously enough — and are treating me as a 'director' at once! It now remains to get some order into everything — to leave time for painting and so on.

Letter to Cicely Jennings / n.d. (1934)

I have just had such a day — learning to 'cut' film, reading scripts watching projections in the theatre, visiting the new GPO studios at Blackheath (very nice) — watching cameramen at work at the Wimpole St Sorting Office (a film about lost letters —) and so on. I am working immediately under Stuart [Legg]'s eye and to some extent 'with' Cavalcanti which all seems promising & certainly it is very exhilarating stuff. Also not particularly strenuous and the people extremely pleasant.

Letter to Cicely Jennings / n.d. (1934)

11

1935. Still working and living in Blackheath, Jennings directed with Len Lye, a New Zealand film animator, **The Birth of the Robot**, an advertising film in colour for Shell-Mex and BP. Jennings also appeared in Stuart Legg's film about the work of the BBC: *BBC — The Voice of Britain*. He contributed an essay on the theatre to a book edited by Geoffrey Grigson, *The Arts Today*. His second daughter was born in August.

2

Making **The Birth of the Robot**

Collage with dog / JD23

Culture

There are still certain things in England that have just not been culturised: examples beer ads; steam railways; Woolworths; clairvoyantes (the backs of playing-cards having been adorned with 'good' patterns lately, someone wanted the faces beautified also). When the life has been finally veneered out of these it really will be the end.

H.J. / Extract from *The Arts Today* / edited by Geoffrey Grigson / Bodley Head / 1935

Reports

The Oaks

The conditions for this race, the most important of the Classic races for three-year-old fillies, were ideal, for the weather was fine and cool. About one o'clock the Aurora again appeared over the hills in a south direction presenting a brilliant mass of light. Once again Captain Allison made a perfect start, for the field was sent away well for the first time that they approached the tapes. It was always evident that the most attenuated light of the Aurora sensibly dimmed the stars, like a thin veil drawn over them. We frequently listened for any sound proceeding from this phenomenon, but never heard any.

1935

13

Racehorses / [c.1933] / JD394

Racehorses / repr. from *London Bulletin*

The Funeral of a Nobleman

This nobleman's career may be likened to a wintry sun, which shines between storms and sets suddenly in gloom.

The apartment in which he expired is distinguished by an awning in front of the window.

It was a delightful sunny day. The enthusiasm was immense. At Parkside the engines stopped to take water. Mr Huskisson having got down from his carriage, the Duke beckoned him to his side and they were just shaking hands when a cry went up from the horrified spectators who perceived that the body was that of Lord Byron being carried to Newstead. Reason never recovered from the hideous coincidence. The journey was completed amidst a deluge of hostile rain and thunder, missiles being hurled at the coach in which the Duke was riding.

From the tomb seawards may be seen Brighton afar off, Worthing nearer, and closer in, in the valley, the village of Salvington.

H.J. / from *Contemporary Poetry and Prose* / edited by Roger Roughton / June 1936

1936. Jennings was a member, together with Herbert Read, André Breton, Roland Penrose and others, of the Organising Committee of the International Surrealist Exhibition which opened at the New Burlington Galleries, London in June and ran for a month. He contributed to *Contemporary Poetry and Prose*, edited by Roger Roughton, both his own material (poems and prose 'Reports') and translated poems by Paul Eluard and E.L.T.Mesens, describing himself at the time as someone who had 'survived the Theatre and English Literature at Cambridge (and) is connected with colour film direction and racehorses'.

In the autumn of 1936 Jennings, together with Stuart Legg, David Gascoyne and Charles Madge discussed the need for an 'anthropology of our own people' — a subject which had arisen out of the crisis over the Simpson divorce and King Edward VIII's impending abdication. This was the genesis of Mass Observation.

14

Surrealism

To the real poet the front of the Bank of England may be as excellent a site for the appearance of poetry as the depths of the sea. Note the careful distinction made by Breton in his article [in *Surrealism*]: 'Human psychism in its most universal aspect has found in the Gothic castle and its accessories a point of fixation so precise that it becomes *essential to discover what would be the equivalent for our own period*' (my italics — H.J.). He continues to say that Surrealism has replaced the 'coincidence' for the 'apparition' and that we must 'allow ourselves to be guided towards the unknown by this newest *promise*'. Now that is talking; and to settle Surrealism down as Romanticism only is to deny this promise. It is to cling to the apparition with its special 'haunt'. It is to look for ghosts only on the battlements, and on battlements only for ghosts. 'Coincidences' have the infinite freedom of appearing anywhere, anytime, to anyone: in broad daylight to those whom we most despise in places we have most loathed: not even to *us* at all: probably least to petty seekers after mystery and poetry on deserted sea-shores and in misty junk-shops.

[. . .] But for the English to awaken from the sleep of selectivity what a task. And to be already a 'painter', a 'writer', an 'artist', a 'surrealist' what a handicap.

H.J. / Review of *Surrealism* edited by Herbert Read,
in *Contemporary Poetry and Prose* / December 1936

From *London Bulletin* / June 1938 / translation, E.L.T.Mesens

PROSE POEM
by
Humphrey Jennings

As the sun declined the snow at our feet reflected the most delicate peach-blossom.

As it sank the peaks to the right assumed more definite, darker and more gigantic forms.

The hat was over the forehead, the mouth and chin buried in the brown velvet collar of the greatcoat. I looked at him wondering if my grandfather's eyes had been like those.

While the luminary was vanishing the horizon glowed like copper from a smelting furnace.

When it had disappeared the ragged edges of the mist shone like the in-equalities of a volcano.

Down goes the window and out go the old gentleman's head and shoulders, and there they stay for I suppose nearly nine minutes.

Such a sight, such a chaos of elemental and artificial lights I never saw nor expect to see. In some pictures I have recognised similar effects. Such are *The Fleeting Hues of Ice* and *The Fire* which we fear to touch.
1937.

POÈME EN PROSE   Par HUMPHREY JENNINGS

Lorsque le soleil déclina la neige à nos pieds reflétait les fleurs de pêcher les plus délicates.

Lorsqu'il se coucha les sommets à la droite accusaient des formes plus définies, plus sombres et plus gigantesques.

Le chapeau était sur le front, la bouche et le menton enfouis dans le col de velours brun du grand manteau. Je le regardai en m'interrogeant si les yeux de mon grand-père étaient comme ceux-là.

Pendant que le foyer s'évanouissait l'horizon s'embrasait comme le cuivre du haut fourneau.

Quand il eut disparu les bords râpés de la brume brillaient comme les inégalités d'un volcan.

Chute de la fenêtre et le vieux, tête et épaules, se penche. Il reste ainsi pour—j'imagine—quelque neuf minutes.

Jamais je n'ai vu, jamais je ne verrai une telle splendeur, un tel chaos de lumières élémentaires et artificielles. Dans certaines peintures j'ai reconnu des effets similaires. Tels sont *Les teintes fuyantes de la glace* et *Le feu* auquel nous n'osons pas toucher.

(traduction par e. l. t. M.)

8

Photograph of own 'Swiss roll' collage / JD33

London in the 17th Century / 1936 / JD10

15

Photograph: paintings in room / JD16

E.L.T.Mesens, Roland Penrose, André Breton
and Jennings at the International Surrealist Exhibition
in London, 1936

Table lyrique / 1936 / JD200

1937. In January Jennings, Tom Harrisson, the anthropologist recently returned from work in the New Hebrides, and Charles Madge, at that time a journalist on the *Daily Mirror*, wrote to the *New Statesman and Nation* setting out the aims of Mass Observation. In April Jennings wrote a Mass Observer's report on himself and in September *May 12th*, the reports of Mass Observers on Coronation Day, was published, edited by Jennings and Charles Madge. In October he had a one man show of paintings at the London Gallery, run by E.L.T.Mesens, and in December gave a talk on *Plagiarism in Poetry* on the BBC.

16

Montage by Jennings of own Coronation Day photographs / MLJ

Mass Observation

Man is the last subject of scientific investigation. A century ago Darwin focussed the camera of thought on to man as a sort of animal whose behaviour and history would be explained by science. In 1847, Marx formulated a scientific study of economic man. In 1865, Tylor defined the new science of anthropology which was to be applied to the 'primitive' and the 'savage'. In 1893, Freud and Breuer published their first paper on hysteria; they began to drag into daylight the unconscious elements in individual 'civilised' man. But neither anthropology nor psychology has yet become more than an instrument in the hands of any individual, which he applies (according to his individuality) to primitives and abnormals.

By 1936 chaos was such that the latent elements were crystallised into a new compound. As so often happens, an idea was being worked out in many separate brains. A letter in *The New Statesman and Nation* from Geoffrey Pyke, arising out of the Simpson crisis, explicitly mentioned the need for an 'anthropology of our own people'. A fortnight later a letter called attention to a group centred in London for the purpose of developing a science of Mass Observation, and this group effected contact with other individuals and with a group working in industrial Lancashire, which had so far concentrated on field work rather than formulation of theory. These interests are now united in the first, necessarily tentative, efforts of Mass Observation.

Mass Observation develops out of anthropology, psychology, and the sciences which study man — but it plans to work with a mass of observers. Already we have fifty observers at work on two sample problems. We are further working out a complete plan of campaign, which will be possible when we have not fifty but 5,000 observers. The following are a few examples of problems that will arise:

Behaviour of people at war memorials
Shouts and gestures of motorists
The aspidistra cult
Anthropology of football pools
Bathroom behaviour
Beards, armpits, eyebrows
Anti-semitism
Distribution, diffusion and significance of the dirty joke
Funerals and undertakers
Female taboos about eating
The private lives of midwives

[. . .] It does not set out in quest of truth or facts for their own sake, or for the sake of an intellectual minority, but aims at exposing them in simple terms to all observers, so that their environment may be understood and thus constantly transformed. Whatever the political methods called upon to effect the transformation, the knowledge of what has to be transformed is indispensable. The foisting on the mass of ideals or ideas developed by men apart from it, irrespective of its capacities, causes mass misery, intellectual despair and an international shambles.

We hope shortly to produce a pamphlet outlining a programme of action. We welcome criticism and co-operation.

Letter to the *New Statesman and Nation*
signed by Tom Harrisson, Humphrey Jennings and Charles Madge / 30 January 1937

Photograph of allotments [Bolton?] /JD59

Painting of allotments / 1944-45 / JD20

17

Extract from a Report

April 12 was a reasonably normal day as my life is at present: it was typical of existence for the last month or so. My health was normal; that is to say I was not more tired headachey or irritable than usual. The weather depended principally on varying densities of high cirrus clouds: thick and even in the early morning, producing a dull foggy effect. Then thinner and more patchy as the day increased until there was bright sun for ten-minute periods in the afternoon. Rather more clouds again in the late afternoon when it was colder. Dull evening but without fog or rain.

No definite dream remembered, but a half-waking thought of something satisfactory (the contrary of waking up worried). Woke up earlier or more easily than usual about 7.45. [. . .] Did teeth while bathwater was running: put too much mouth wash into mug: have a tendency to do this as too much produces a

THEY SPEAK FOR THEMSELVES
MASS OBSERVATION AND SOCIAL NARRATIVE

[*The reports which are written for Mass Observation come largely from people whose lives are spent in a world whose behaviour, language, and viewpoint are far removed from academic science and literature. Sociologists and realistic novelists—including proletarian novelists—find it difficult if not impossible to describe the texture of this world. After reading hundreds of Mass Observation reports, we find that they tend to cover just those aspects of life which the others miss. Why is this? Because, we suggest, in these reports people are speaking in a language natural to them—their spelling, punctuation, etc., are their* OWN—*in spite of a uniform State education. This is hardly a " well of English undefiled " since into it continually flow more or less muddy streams from press, radio, advertising, film, and " literature ". But in actual social usage, all the jungle of words grow up together in Darwinian conflict until they establish their own ecology and functions. Contrast this functional value with the use of words by sensitive, stylist writers. Each phrase is paralysed by fear of cliché. Yet each phrase must have a class or family resemblance to one of the known accents of literature. In reaction against this paralysis, there is a general wish among writers to be* UNLIKE *the intellectual,* LIKE *the masses. Much " proletarian fiction " is a product of this wish. But it is not enough for such fiction to be* ABOUT *proletarians, if they in their turn become a romantic fiction, nor even for it to be* BY *proletarians, if it is used by them as a means of escaping out of the proletariat.*

Mass Observation is among other things giving working-class and middle class people a chance to speak for themselves, about themselves. How little they are affected by the paralysis of language, even in their first attempts, may be judged from the extracts from Mass Observation reports which follow.]

C. M. and H. J.

18

'kick' like a neat spirit. [. . .] Remembered I should try to look tidy as I had to deal with new typist first job this morning. Noticed Hardy's poems lying on floor of bedroom: had read some night before. Had brought 'Daily Mirror' in from hall on way back from bath; sat and read it half dressed on edge of bed. [. . .] Met a strange man coming out of Ch.'s [Madge] as I went in. Went round to back to let myself in. Crossing loggia noticed contrast of bicycles, old boxes and rubbish with sunny garden seen through round-headed arches. Nearly photographed one arch as I have experience that in photographing from shadow through an arch into sunlight a curious optical effect is produced . . . Wandered into churchyard to take photo of tombs: as I was using filter I had to wait a long time for really good sun. Shot no good in the end because while waiting for sun I was afraid someone would come and complain of my photographing in churchyard. Walked again. Arrived about 2.30. As I rang bell I thought 'I suppose photography has to get more and more realistic as one gets older.' [. . .] At 4.30 Charles said J was coming at 5 and he (Ch) wished to discuss with me scientific aspect of M.O. We walked over the Heath. . . We walked across grass to Greenwich park. Ch. good on Lenin and table: I connected what he said about contemporary psychology with Nelson I suppose from looking down on Royal Naval Hospital.

Report written by H.J./ 12 April 1937

Graveyard (negative print) / JD44

Poem, based on a book of photographs
by Walker Evans

Philadelphia

*Let us in imagination turn our
            faces westward*

*The green cars of the Union line running out
                                    Ninth Street*

The red cars of the Second running out Third Street
The yellow cars of the Eastern Penitentiary
The white marble of the prime Methodist
The rich brown of First Baptist
The splendid Episcopal church of the Incarnation
The pioneers of the prime homes
*The pleasant spots in which repose the
                dead of this great city*

(May 1936)

Three American Poems

The hills are like the open downs of England — the peaceful herds upon the grassy slopes, the broken sea-washed cliffs, the beach with ever-tumbling surf, the wrecks that strew the shore in pitiful reminder, the crisp air from the sea, the long superb stretch of blue waters — the Graveyard.

As we journey up the valley
Of the Connecticut
The swift thought of the locomotive
Recovers the old footprints.

Even in this desolate country, where neither trees nor verdure dressed, and, as they supposed, of uninhabitable terror, like us above the birds, like us above the fishes, like us above the insects, singing and dancing, a man.

1938

The Origin of Colour / 1937 / JD61

* Charles Laughton played the title roles in *Ruggles of Red Gap* (Leo McCarey, 1935), *Rembrandt* (Alexander Korda, 1936) and *The Beachcomber* (alias *Vessel of Wrath*, Erich Pommer, 1938).

Who Does That Remind You Of ?

Two or three years ago there seems to have been a plan for taking the glass off the pictures in the National Gallery, so that you could see *them* instead of a reflection of yourself. Also important as breaking down a barrier between the public and the 'sacredness' of the images they are allowed to peer at. The glass having in fact been taken off a Honthorst (a big Dutch picture) I asked the attendant if they were seriously going to take the glass off all the pictures. He said he certainly hoped *not*. Why? because he'd have a terrible time: 'do you know what they do? They come in here and put their hands over the mouth and nose of a Rembrandt, and then say 'Who does *that* remind you of?''.'

No doubt the appearance of Rembrandt in this kind of story (rather than say Titian) is due to his connections with photography; — 'Rembrandt lighting', sepia prints (in imitation of Rembrandt's colouring), his etchings (the photography of his time — exploited as competition with 19th century photography by Whistler), the suburban photographer's studio called 'Rembrandt House' (fact) — i.e. portrait photography ('who does that remind you of?') etc. Then of late we have had Mr Laughton as Rembrandt philosophically reading the Old Testament — before that as Ruggles as Lincoln, and since as a beachcomber* — in fact it is clear that Rembrandt (particularly in his pictures of 'Philosophers') was one of the first people to exploit the 'Old Curiosity Shop' motif, and with it all the different ideas coming under the heading of a 'brown study'.

Photography itself — 'photogenic drawing' — began simply as the mechanisation of realism, and it remains *the* system with which the people can be

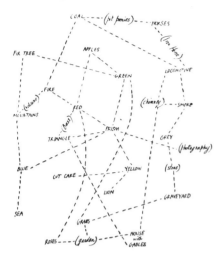

pictured by the people for the people: simple to operate, results capable of mass reproduction and circulation, effects generally considered truthful ('the camera cannot lie') and so on. But intellectually the importance of the camera lies clearly in the way in which it deals with problems of choice — choice and avoidance of choice. Freud (*Psychopathology of Everyday Life*, Chapter 12) says that the feeling of Déjà Vu ('Who does that remind you of?') 'corresponds to the memory of an unconscious fantasy'. The camera is precisely an instrument for recording the object or image that prompted that memory. Hence the rush to see 'how they came out'.

In the same book Freud insists on the impossibility of a voluntarily 'arbitrary' choice or association of objects. Below is an unfinished (or incomplete) chart of certain words and images (evidently a personal list) with dotted-line indications of the relationships ordinarily assumed to exist between them (between 'sea' and 'blue' for instance). Clearly it is a problem just how far these 'common sense' relationships differ from or overlap the relationships (between 'prism' and 'fir tree' for example) established in a painting or dictated by 'unconscious fantasy'.

From *London Bulletin* / October 1938

20

Tableau parisien / 1938-39 / JD108

The Origin of Colour / 1937 / JD113

1938. Jennings gave another talk, *The Disappearance of Ghosts*, on the radio in February and was commissioned by the BBC to work on a series on *The Poet and the Public*, starting with talks on the nature of poetry and the poet's relationship with his public and going on to discussions with poets: C. Day Lewis, Herbert Read, Patience Strong. During the year he directed two films for the GPO Film Unit: **Penny Journey**, tracing the journey of a picture postcard, and **Speaking from America**.

Locomotive / [c.1936] / Stuart Legg

Tableaux Parisiens

People going to look at a Rembrandt — what is there about a Rembrandt?

Choice of Images — *Déjà vu*: the images on this list related to the phenomenon of *déjà vu* in the sense in which Freud explains this phenomenon — the image fulfilling the already existent fantasy. The relation of *déjà vu* to 'reincarnation', 'spirals in time' and other such complexities is due to the fantasy being related to a special scene or object — i.e. the actual scene is imagined to have happened before. But the sensation of *déjà vu* before an image or to a serial object (an object produced in series such as an apple, a rose, a locomotive) precludes all idea of such rubbish. The use therefore of images and serial objects is important as a debunking of idealism and furthers the cause of materialism. Further confronted with an image (a photo or an engraving) a far more detached analysis is possible than with a scene which in many cases is only passed through (in a car or a train) and is in other ways unpossessable — unavailable for detached analysis. But with an image the parts of the image which correspond to the fantasy can be separated from those which do not.

Example: Some years ago (say 1930-1934) I bought in Cambridge a few 19th-century etchings in Paris: thinking vaguely that they reminded me of the areas on the left bank (quai Voltaire etc) which were gradually being knocked down — I never studied them in detail. To roughly the same period belongs a detailed study of Baudelaire's poems of which the sections named *Tableaux Parisiens* have always particularly moved me, representing a nostalgia also for Paris — and *Le Cygne* in particular. Reading poetry in Paris I connect with a café on the right bank — where I first read Rimbaud — opposite the Place Voltaire — facing the Louvre. *Le Cygne* makes a definite reference to the destruction of the Place Carrousel (in 1848 and onwards) for the rebuilding of the Louvre:

> Andromaque, je pense à vous! Ce petit fleuve,
> Pauvre et triste miroir où jadis resplendit
> L'immense majesté de vos douleurs de veuve,
> Ce Simoïs menteur qui par vos pleurs grandit,
>
> A fécondé soudain ma mémoire fertile,
> Comme je traversais le nouveau Carrousel.
> Le vieux Paris n'est plus (la forme d'une ville
> Change plus vite, hélas! que le coeur d'un mortel).*

* From 'Le Cygne' (1859), by Charles Baudelaire

Unpublished n.d.

1939. Early in the year he moved to 19 St James's Gardens, London W11 and from the end of March worked on location in the North of England on the making of **Spare Time** (at that time provisionally titled *British Workers*), a film which drew directly on his Mass Observation work, although he himself had now moved on from Mass Observation itself.

In July he was on location in the Mediterranean making **S.S.Ionian** (or *Her Last Trip*) a film on a trip made by a Merchant Navy ship. In August he returned to the GPO Film Unit and after the outbreak of war made **The First Days** and **Spring Offensive.**

Grove Farm

A derelict cart with dead grass entwined in its great wheels: plants and grasses which had climbed in the springtime and been upheld by the spokes, flowered in the summer and now died in October. The cart unmoved all the year round — the wheels unmoved and unmoving — lit and unlit with the daily light of the great sun . . .

Autumn 1939

Moonlight '39

December 1939 — coming back from a Christmas dinner with Paule Vézelay, in bright moonlight the meaningless architecture of Earl's Court Road looks like the facade of an Italian Palace. At midnight outside the Underground station a barrel-organ playing the 'Blue Danube'.

The Making of 'Spare Time'

Then after Derby up into the Peak district — quite new to me — where the pubs are painted like early Ben Nicholsons: coloured lettering LIKE THIS [see illustration] and the edges of the houses in pink. And right up on the top of the hills lime works blowing white dust on the moors: not unconnected with BN now. Mixture of mist and hardness. Buxton looking very smug: and then the beginning of Cotton at Stockport. Cotton seems to produce a desolation greater — more extended — than any other industry. From Stockport it is really all streets through Manchester, Bolton, Preston — almost to the sea at Blackpool — about 60 miles. The desolation — the peculiar kind of human misery which it expresses comes I think from the fact that 'Cotton' simply means *work*: Spinning what is produced or grown elsewhere in America or India. Coal and Steel at least suggest something produced on the spot. At Manchester there was a sort of thin wet sunlight which makes it look pathetic. It has á grim sort of fantasy. And a certain dignity of its own from being connected with certain events in history.

Letter to Cicely Jennings / 21 March 1939

This is a vast, hot crazy hotel — which stands right up above Sheffield and certainly has the most wonderful views of factory chimneys and waste land and railway lines — Railways — I see *La Bête Humaine* is coming to the Paris Cinema in a day or two and is all about railways.

Letter to Cicely Jennings / 13 April 1939

Bright sun & huge white clouds and patches of rain — with a rainbow and circling pigeons. We also photographed men buying 6d postal orders for football pools — they sell about 7,000 every Friday at the P.O. here.

Letter to Cicely Jennings / 14 April 1939

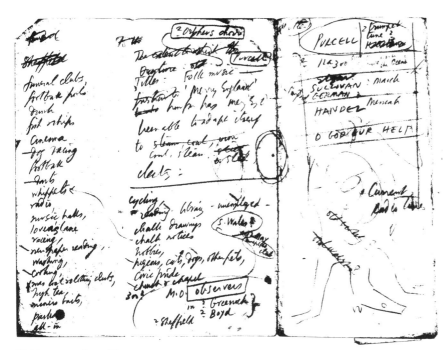

Working notes on **Spare Time** images

1

2

3

4

Spare Time is a film about working-class leisure. It was shot in South-East Lancashire (mainly Manchester, Salford and Bolton), Sheffield and South Wales (mainly Pontypridd). The sound-track consists largely of music, much of it on screen. There is a little natural sound, and a very sparse commentary (spoken by Laurie Lee):
'This is a film about the way people spend their spare time, people in three British industries — steel, cotton and coal.'
'Between work and sleep comes the time we call our own. What do we do with it?'
(Framestill **1**)

'Steel: the three-shift system means that the steelworker's spare time may come in the morning, or in the afternoon.'
(Framestills **2-7**)
'Cotton: the mills open at eight and close at five; Saturday afternoons and Sundays are off.' (Framestills **8-11**)
'And finally, coal.' (Framestills **12-15**)
'As things are, spare time is a time when we have a chance to do what we like, a chance to be most ourselves.' (Framestill **16**)

5

9

13

24

6

10

14

7

11

15

8

12

16

The Blitz/'Listen to Britain'/'Fires Were Started'
Lidice and Wales /'Diary for Timothy'

1940. In the early part of 1940, Jennings worked on **Spring Offensive, Welfare of the Workers** and **London Can Take It** (with Harry Watt) — all films to demonstrate Britain's ability to survive during the blitz and, after the fall of France, in Europe alone. **London Can Take It** was aimed specifically at the Empire and American market. The GPO Film Unit was transferred to the Ministry of Information and Cavalcanti left, to be replaced by Ian Dalrymple. After his family left for America in September, Jennings started work on **Heart of Britain** — a complement to the city-based **London Can Take It** about the country and towns of Britain during wartime.

London, October 1940

[. . .] coming across Leicester Square just after the sirens there are two French soldiers, talking. The three quarter moonface very bright with a few streaks of cloud. A group of white faces outside Lyons looking up watching a great balloon sailing into the sky. Then in the shadow a man with a street piano fingering a prelude. The officers cross over. The guns begin to thud. The balloon rises fast across the luminous clouds. The moon is bright enough to cast long shadows. The piano begins to play 'Land of Hope and Glory — Mother of the Free'.

The Blitz, 1940

You left you remember on a Friday night in an alert as we now call them. The next morning was quiet enough: very fine and bright, we were working at Blackheath as usual — then quite suddenly at almost 4 in the afternoon the blitz began: the studio of course right in the line of it. The boys of course were terrific — saved the negative from an incendiary on the roof — went out all night photographing the fires.[. . .] Well after that first burst of blitz they decided some of our work could be done out of town and as Dalrymple had come to take Cav's place and I was pretty tired by the end of ten days of it — he asked me to come down for the weekend. [. . .]

After the first fortnight we began to work on film-reporting of the blitz and are now up to our eyes in it — first pic. 'London Can Take It' specially for you in the States! I am in Liverpool just for a moment on a kind of 'Spare Time' assignment. [. . .]

Some of the damage in London is pretty heart-breaking but what an effect it has had on the people! What warmth — what courage! what determination. People sternly encouraging each other by explaining that when you hear a bomb whistle it means it has missed you! People in the north singing in public shelters: 'One man went to mow — went to mow a meadow.' WVS girls serving hot drinks to firefighters during raids explaining that really they are 'terribly afraid all the time!' [. . .] Everybody absolutely determined: secretly delighted with the *privilege* of holding up Hitler. Certain of beating him: a certainty which no amount of bombing can weaken, only strengthen.[. . .] Maybe by the time you get this one or two more 18th cent. churches will be smashed up in London: some civilians killed: some personal loves and treasures wrecked — but it means nothing; a curious kind of unselfishness is developing which can stand all that and more. We have found ourselves on the right side and on the right track at last!

Letter to Cicely Jennings / 20 October 1940

London Can Take It (production still)

Heart of Britain (production still)

London Can Take It

[. . .] which we (GPO) made for the Ministry that Harry[Watt] and self directing — plus Jonah [Jones], Chick [Fowle] and McAllister cutting — plus of course the terrific luck of using Quentin Reynolds' commentary. [. . .] And the war? well we feel we aren't doing too badly: in fact there is a kind of secret exultation. You know I have always said the war was a moral problem for the English.

Letter to Cicely Jennings / 3 November 1940

Heart of Britain: 1940

Everything seems much as usual: we have had a few exciting nights in the Midlands but not much else. The hills and valleys of the North are as quiet as ever and the pubs and dance halls are fuller and brighter than before: entertainment has moved North.

[. . .] Since writing the above there has been the grim attack on Coventry which I am glad to say we were not in: we had left there a few days before. But we have very many good friends there and I am at the moment on my way there to find out how things really are. The voluntary workers there — canteen girls and others — we had been photographing and had been out at night in the canteen washing up mugs and making tea. A superb group of people: sweet young kids and magnificent women: How are they?

Letter to Cicely Jennings / 12 November 1940 / Penrith

Picture: The 'Midi' Symphony

Picture an English interior in the remotest village of Oxfordshire: a mother, a married daughter, the mother of an evacuee, reading and knitting quietly after dinner — the bombers going out from the neighbouring airfield while the radio plays the pathetic music of Haydn. On the walls are portraits, photographs, watercolours, of men — predominantly men — engineers and soldiers, going back to the days of Robert Stephenson and the Crimea — little framed fragments of regimental colours — photographs of railway bridges — men in uniform and men as children.

How beautiful Haydn — what measure — what warmth of brass — what tears of strings — what march of ensemble — what forgiveness. Children of the grown-ups here listening and reading — children upstairs asleep. What a nostalgia the penultimate movement of the 'Midi' symphony. Outside in the dark the corn ripens: it is the last day in July. The trumpets of Haydn call us. The bombers are all gone. The sky is clear. The flutes in the last movement thrill us. The ears of corn move for a moment. The knitting-needles click. The trumpets return. The bombers are already over the white coast-line.

July-August 1940

Words for Battle

We follow Wavell in Libya, think a little more seriously of our gas-masks and agree with the German radio that we are on the verge of historic something or others: we also know that the other day an old lady of ninety-odd by herself tore down the wall paper with her bare hands and put out a fire-bomb. That children playing in the streets lie flat on their faces when they hear bombs falling and then get up and go on playing — that people are singing Handel and listening to Beethoven as never before.

Letter to Cicely Jennings / 25 January 1941

Queer life: we were recording Handel's Water Music (of all things) the other night at the Queen's Hall with the LPO — and the sound comes out from the loudspeaker with the sound-truck in the street. Near the end of the session there were 'chandelier' flares overhead — lighting up the sky — the music echoing down the street: the planes booming and the particular air-raid sound: people kicking broken glass on the pavement.

[. . .] I have been accused of 'going religious' for putting the Hallelujah Chorus at the end of 'This is England' [**Words for Battle**]. This of course from Rotha and other of Grierson's little boys who are still talking as loudly as possible about 'pure documentary' and 'realism' and other such systems of self-advertisement.

Letter to Cicely Jennings / March 1941

27

1941. Early in the year he began **Words for Battle**, working on location mainly in London and having moved out to Ian Dalrymple's house near Pinewood during the blitz. **Words for Battle** juxtaposed words and pictures to show what Britain was fighting for. Jennings suggested that a film might be made showing how Hitler had betrayed the German ideal expressed by Goethe and Heine but this came to nothing. In February he broadcast on the French Service of the BBC as part of a series on *Pourquoi j'aime la France*. By June he had started on **Listen to Britain**, filming on location in London, Manchester, Blackpool and the Lake District. In October, at the end of the work on **Listen to Britain**, which he made jointly with Stewart McAllister, his editor, he commenced writing the first treatment of a film on the work of the National Fire Service — to become **Fires Were Started.**

Opening shot of **Words for Battle**

Words for Battle is divided into seven sections, followed by a 'coda'. Each section consists of a sequence of related or contrasting images, accompanied by a commentary read by Laurence Olivier in voice over.

The texts used for the commentary are:

1. Camden's *Description of Britain*
2. Milton, *Areopagitica*
3. Blake, *Jerusalem*
4. Browning, *Home-Thoughts, from the Sea*
5. Kipling, *The Beginnings*
6. Churchill, Speech of 4 June 1940
7. Lincoln, Gettysburg Address

The coda (**8**) consists of a tracking shot, accompanied only by music (Handel's 'Water Music').

The framestills reproduced here are designed to illustrate the relation of sound to image, either within a sequence (**2**, **3** and **6**), across a cut (**5**), or over the duration of a single shot (**7**).

2

'I see her as an eagle...'

'... the noise of timorous and flocking birds'

3

'I will not cease...'

'Till we have built...'

4

'Sunset ran, one glorious blood-red'

5

'When time shall count from the date'

'When the English began to hate'

6

'We shall go on to the end...'

'We shall never surrender'

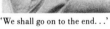

7 'And that government of the people
by the people and for the people. . .'

'. . . shall not perish from the earth'

8

1942. Location shooting on the Fire Service film began in February and continued through to April. In June, the Germans massacred the citizens of the mining village of Lidice, Czechoslovakia and it was suggested to the Ministry of Information, possibly by the Czech government in exile, that a film be made to commemorate the village, which had been totally obliterated. In August, Jennings went to Wales to look for a suitable location and settled on the mining village of Cwmgiedd, near Ystradgynlais. By the beginning of September, Jennings and his unit had moved into Cwmgiedd and were living with mining families, rather than in a local hotel, and location shooting in Wales was completed by the end of the year. His return to London coincided with a major row on a proposal to cut **Fires Were Started** drastically, in order to conform with the demands of the commercial distributors.

London 1942

London has settled down to a big village-like existence. Most of the damage demolished and cleared up. Endless allotments — beds of potatoes, onions and lettuces in parks, in the new open spaces from bombing, tomatoes climbing up ruins — trees and shrubs overgrowing evacuated and empty houses and gardens; in some places shells of eighteenth century cottages with black windows and Rousseau-like forest enveloping them, straying out over the road — no railings — climbing in windows.

    Elsewhere the utmost tidiness and care in lines of planting on AA gunsites, aerodromes, fire stations. The parks and gardens open to all, all railings gone. There is of course very widespread exasperation about the Second Front — partly political but more unspoken impatience and shame — the more so because the country realises that it has been working hard and sacrificing. I should theoretically be very tired at the end of a picture but I don't think I do: I don't think it's work so much as war . . . or maybe it's middle-age but I don't feel middle-aged, on the contrary — younger than ever. There is nothing so exhilarating as seeing even a few ideas one has long had really coming into being on the screen.

Letter to Cicely Jennings / 28 July 1942

Listen to Britain

[. . .] It is half-past nine — the children are already at school and the teacher is calling out the orders to a PT class in the playground. Just over the school wall a housewife is washing up the breakfast. The sound of the children comes in through the window. She stops for a moment — looks across to the mantelpiece, to a photo of a boy in a Glengarrie: a great wave of emotion sweeps over her — the sound of the Pipes played not in the hills of Scotland, but in the sand dunes of Syria, where her lad is away at the war. And then she comes back to the washing up, and the kids in the playground go on with their PT.

All over Britain, the morning's work is now in full swing: and at 10.30 the BBC comes 'Calling All Workers', and in the factories all over the land half-an-hour of 'Music While You Work' peps up production: the production of the tools for finishing the job.

At half-past twelve, the clatter of typing in the Ministries and offices in London lessens as the girls begin to break for lunch. And in the centre of the City wartime Londoners are crowding up the steps of the National Gallery for what has become one of the most popular creations of the War: the lunchtime concerts. Inside, in one of the great galleries, where the visitor in peacetime used to tip-toe and whisper and admire, now there sit a thousand Londoners, in and out of uniform, who have come from homes and works and offices to hear the music of Mozart. And sitting among them the Queen. The music is in uniform too — played by the Central Band of the Royal Air Force.

After all the blitzes, London still remains a strong and noble and beautiful city, and she is not being left in ruins. Facing St Paul's, giant cranes swing metal girders high up over the traffic, and in a thousand places inside its huge circumference, London is being rebuilt in the sunlight.

Now the boom of the traffic is pierced by the shrill of fifes of the Marines' Band, and they in their turn are drowned by the tremendous rhythms of industry: the screaming of the cold chisel, the pounding of the steam hammer. And now in a factory canteen, the roar of working-men's voices, and the clatter of spoons and metal plates applaud the profoundest clowns in the country: Flanagan & Allen. Then, as the final music builds up, the afternoon shifts put their backs into it, and the twenty-four hours of life in Britain that we have just seen will have played their full part in The Tin Hat Concerto.

From a Treatment for **Listen to Britain**, entitled 'The Tin Hat Concerto' / August 1941

Listen to Britain

'Fires Were Started'

[. . .] in Stepney and Wapping on the Fire picture. We have more or less taken over a small district, roped off streets, organised the locals and so on. It has been exceptionally hard and tiring work . . . supplies of all sorts very short.

But of course the place and the people illuminating beyond everything. The river, the wharves and shipping, the bridge in Wapping Lane smelling permanently of cinnamon, the remains of Chinatown, the *Prospect of Whitby* and another wonderful pub called the *Artichoke* which is our field Headquarters. Reconstruction of a fire in the docks.

A charming Fire-station at a school in the centre of Wellclose Square which for all the world looks like Vermeer's view of Delft. Ridiculous plaster rococo cherubs on the front of a blitzed house, an old man who comes and plays the flute superbly well on Fridays, Mr Miller who owns a chain of antique shops and specialises in Crown Derby, Jock who runs the Sailors Mission, Wapping Church mentioned in Pepys which we are using for a fireman's funeral. And the people themselves, firemen and others: T.P.Smith ex-international banquet waiter — Fred Griffiths ex taxi-driver — Loris Rey ex Glasgow School of Art — Sadie the girl at the Artichoke — Mr C at the warehouse who upset a precious bottle of Soir de Paris all over the safe and then insisted on drenching everybody's hankies in it — and what the Sub-Officer's wife said when he came home smelling like that.

For the last two months we have been working at this down there for twelve hours a day six days a week: we are now roughly half way through and pretty exhausted: the results peculiar and very unlike anything I have had to do with before: popular, exciting, funny — mixture of slapstick and macabre blitz reconstruction.[. . .]

It has now become 14 hours a day — living in Stepney the whole time — really have never worked so hard at anything or I think thrown myself into anything so completely. Whatever the results it is definitely an advance in film making for me — really beginning to understand people and making friends with them and not just looking at them and lecturing or pitying them. Another general effect of the war.

. . . Painting etc. I am afraid I haven't touched for months now — but maybe when this pic. is finished I shall get back to a little. Reading nothing. Life concerned with a burning roof — smoke fire water — men's faces and thoughts: a tangle of hose, orders shouted in the dark — falling walls, brilliant moonlight — dust, mud, tiredness until nobody is quite sure where the film ends and the conditions of making it begin: a real fire could not be more tiring and certainly less trouble. But what one learns at midnight with tired firemen. . .

Letter to Cicely Jennings / 12 April 1942

31

Detail from a group photograph taken during the making of **Fires Were Started**

Top row: Graham Wallace, two firemen
Middle row: Nora Dawson,
Humphrey Jennings, Stewart McAllister,
C. Pennington Richards
Bottom left: Sadie Cohen

Fires Were Started (production still)

Making **Fires Were Started**

Fires Were Started (production still)

First View of Cwmgiedd / August 1942

You get to Cwmgiedd by crossing over — out of the town, straggly houses and so on — round the corner — you come to a coal canal — one of the old canals that they used for getting the coal down to Swansea and Cardiff before the railways came in and there was a bridge over the coal canal; and the coal canal sort of cuts the village off from Ystradgynlais and from the rest of the country and up in a little valley, there is the village of Cwmgiedd, with a little straight street that goes up into the hill and on each side — charming, beautiful little stone houses and down the middle, parallel to the street, is a mountain stream that comes running down — with a little water in the summer as we saw it and then as we got to know it in the autumn and the winter with floods coming down when the snow is up on the Black Mountains. And half way up is a grocer's shop on the right — Tom Powell, Family Grocer, and on the left, a beautiful white Methodist Chapel — the Chapel of Yorath — the name of the original village. Because Cwmgiedd actually isn't really a village name — Cwmgiedd means the Valley of the turbulent river. It's a very turbulent river running down this valley and this extraordinarily beautiful group of cottages and then the rest of the street going up — beyond the school and so on — up into the farms and mountains, and way, away up into the woods at the top.

BBC talk by Jennings / 26 May 1943

33

Making **The Silent Village**

Pithead / [c.1943] / JD45

The Silent Village

I really never thought to live to see the honest Christian and Communist principles daily acted on as a matter of course by a large number of British — I won't say English — people living together. Not merely honesty, culture, manners, practical socialism, but real life: with passion and tenderness and comradeship and heartiness all combined. From these people one can really understand Cromwell's New Model Army and the defenders of many places at the beginning of the Industrial Revolution. The people are really Tolstoyan figures — or it is a place where Turgenev's *Lear of the Steppes* could have taken place. We are photographing them as honestly as possible — neither like *How Green* — too theatrical, or *The Grapes of Wrath* — too poverty-stricken.

Letter to Cicely Jennings / 10 September 1942

Absolutely non-stop for nearly three months. On this I feel at least that we have really begun to get close to the men — not just as individuals — but also as a class — with an understanding between us: so they don't feel we are just photographing them as curios or wild animals or 'just for propaganda'. As you probably have seen, a large number of people — especially archbishops and bankers — have started telling us what the country and even the world is to be like after the war — and many of their suggestions surprisingly 'left' or 'socialistic' at first glance, but all equally sure that private profit must stay — nationalisation must be avoided and so on. One can only hope that the people will not be bamboozled the ninetieth time.

Here at this moment — How different and yet also a part with a central motif of its own: a brilliant afternoon — the wind blowing long low black and white clouds over the hills (the Black Mountains) the white smoke and steam from Tireni pit and the steelworks down the valley streaming across with them. Strong clean winter sun on the washing in hundreds of backgardens — the chapel standing up white and looking newly washed — the men in blue with white silk scarves and brown shiny shoes squatting on street corners — three lads home 'dirty' from the morning shift almost lying on the pavement waiting for the Neath Bus. The Children in red woollen hoods coming out of school and walking some of them far up into the hills to little pink-washed farms and lonely cottages. A horse in a front garden. Three geese at the top end of the village. The blacksmith's baby girl with no front teeth — who says 'Hullo Jennings' very aggressively. Dave [Hopkins, in whose house he was living] now back and bathed (he comes home dirty and pops straight into his bath) lying half asleep in front of an anthracite fire. To-night before turning in Mrs Hopkins will roll back the mat and put out his boots and working clothes before the same fire banked up with cinders — so that they shall be warm to put on at 6 to-morrow morning . . . In the meantime take Mrs Hopkins as an average worker today: she is doing no official war-work — the things you see in newsreels and *Mrs Miniver* — all she does is this: she gets up at 6 to see her man off to work — his breakfast and collier's box and so on — then she gets me up at 8 — then she has her own breakfast and begins shopping and cooking for herself and at least two other families — for Jack's family because he has silicosis and his wife works in munitions — for her brother Len — because he works in the Seven (Seven Sisters Pit) and his wife is in rooms — then her sister-in-law Nan comes home from night shift from munitions and wants bath food and sleep. Then lunch for me. Then after lunch Dave comes home — wants bath food and sleep. Then tea for all of us. Then Mary comes in to cook and wash *here*. Then Nan gets up and is off to night shift at 8 (two hours journey there — two hours back — ten hour shift). Then supper and she gets to bed at 11. Fortunately they have no children — some people are doing this with four or five children and or evacuees!

[. . .] In the dark streets now the children are skipping with ropes made of knotted colour rag and calling down the hill. At the bottom of the hill runs the river Giedd over huge stones and talks all night. Inside the kettle is singing and Dave and Mrs are playing cards — a peculiar game whose score is written down on the back of Co-op order forms. Nan is making up her sandwiches for to-night's shift. On the mantlepiece two enormous china dogs stare out at nothing — permanently warm from the tremendous anthracite blaze below them.

Letter to Cicely Jennings / 14 November 1942

Wales in Snow

Have you seen Wales in Snow?
I don't mean on the hills or farms or photographs of Snowdon.
I mean on Dowlais Top and the Merthyr Road
I mean the shift that went down in starlight and worked in the dark and came up in the pale fleece of the afternoon.
I mean this man with thumbs in his belt and his old mac blowing — with the black earth on his face and the white sky on his boots — with only his teeth and eyes whiter than Wales in snow.

1943

The Silent Village (production still)

The Silent Village / the reprisals
(production still)

1943. From January to at least May, Jennings was involved in the editing of **The Silent Village**, the Lidice film. By June he had started on a treatment for a possible film on a history of the Royal Marines — work which was interrupted in July by a 'special mission' to film the invasion of Sicily. Jennings seems to have been away for about six weeks — first filming commando training in Scotland and then the invasion itself. On his return his ideas about the Royal Marines film had radically changed and in the event the film was never started. In October he had begun a film on the popularity of a German song, Lili Marlene, which had been adopted by the Eighth Army in the North African campaign, and by the end of December, shooting of the **Lili Marlene** film had been completed. Also early in 1943 he restarted work on a project for a book about the coming of the Machine, using texts from English writers of the 17th, 18th and 19th centuries. He signed a contract with George Routledge and Sons for a book entitled *Pandaemonium*, the manuscript to be delivered in June. In the event the manuscript was not delivered. Jennings kept adding to the material right until his death. The unpublished manuscript was edited by Charles Madge in 1953 with a view to finding a new publisher, but none was found.

Cutting 'Fires Were Started'

All sorts of people — official and otherwise — who apparently had not had the courage to speak out before suddenly discovered that that was what they had thought all along, that the picture was much too long and much too slow and that really instead of being the finest picture we had produced (which was the general opinion till then) it was a hopeless muddle which could only be 'saved' by being cut right down and so on.

Well of course one expects that from spineless well-known modern novelists and poets who have somehow got into the propaganda business — who have no technical knowledge and no sense of solidarity or moral courage. But worse — the opinion of people at Pinewood began to change. All this arising out of the criticism of one or two people in Wardour Street — who had other irons in the fire anyway and who fight every inch against us trespassing on what they pretend is their field. In the meantime Lejeune of *The Observer* had seen it and said it was easily the finest documentary ever made and that to touch it would be like cutting up Beethoven!

Letter to Cicely Jennings / 18 November 1942

35

Pandaemonium

I have got out again [. . .] the material assembled years back on the Industrial Revolution and [have been] asked to go down to the Swansea valley and give a series of talks to the miners on poetry and the Industrial Revolution which really is a golden opportunity — so doing some work on that I have got as far once again of thinking of it as a book and looking for a publisher and so. Masses of new material — but again no time or very little. . .

Letter to Cicely Jennings / 24 January 1943

German footage with Emmy Goering, incorporated into **The True Story of Lili Marlene**

Invasion of Sicily, July 1943

Away in the wilds first living with a Commando unit, and then going out in convoy, the Mediterranean sun (surprisingly one felt) just as it always was, then watching the landings — the first at night and then by day, and then returning again by sea, via Algiers and Oran and Gib.[. . .] Very exciting really, and prodigiously skilful — really and truly thousands of ships coming up through the narrows to the Sicilian coast — keeping their time and station to a matter of minutes — watching even the moon set just before the landing craft were dropped!

The chaps themselves were really tremendous. Young and on their toes — not at all the popular conception of Commandos as rough-necks. The officers principally ex-intellectuals — a landscape painter, a writer, a man with the Oxford Book in his pocket — chaps extraordinarily like the old GPO boys.[. . .] We did some pretty good shooting I think — but as ever the most exciting and moving stuff quite unphotographable — as the night landing itself (very dangerous as it had been blowing a gale all day and the sea was swamping landing-craft) as the last night in port — the chaps singing 'Goodbye ladies' and — astonishingly enough — 'Who killed Cock Robin' and a miraculous little song beginning 'Ohhh! the little humming bird . . .' Then the church parade held simultaneously by the whole convoy — including lessons from Revelations — the vision of the White Horse.

Letter to Cicely Jennings/3 September 1943

After Stalingrad

We took a packet of bombing in London once upon a time — but as the end of the four years we are extraordinarily lucky — compared to anywhere in Europe itself. What happens in German (and Italian) cities I do not like to imagine. I suppose we shall sort it out sometime. Do not, dearest, in the next year as things get confused and rougher, forget me or let me get further away: the confidence we have got must be there when the fighting stops — sententious as that may sound. No, but I say that because England has you will find, changed a great deal: not so much any one person is different but the young coming up are pretty determined — and people in general if they have the same character have had a good think. The man and woman in the particular job — the ploughman and the coal-cutter and the commando are very definite as to what was wrong five years ago. The present resilience of Russia — the sheer performance — from Stalingrad to Kharkov and beyond has had an effect I think even greater on us than the original heroic resistance and scorched earth. We ourselves were good at taking a beating. But with all due respect to our great 8th Army — the dazzling Russian advances of this summer: done by mere sheer military means — invoking neither winter, nor mud nor snow nor heat nor terrain nor poor allies nor internal collapse — but by the art of war — this has really opened our mouths. I do not think it has been sufficiently appreciated publicly — but in our hearts we know now that not only have the Russians saved us from the Nazis, but also that they are beating them for us all. I hope and trust we shall not forget.

Letter to Cicely Jennings / 3 September 1943

Diary for Timothy

Outside 8 Regents Park Terrace

I Saw Harlequin

I saw Harlequin dancing by the factory chimneys
    Lay your head low on my arm love
And his name was Chartism
    Close your eyes and rest
I saw Harlequin stepping through the machine-shops
    Hold your breath and wait
I saw Harlequin peeping in the fox-holes of Kharkov
    Hold your hand tight in mine
And his name was the Russian guerilla
    Open your eyes and watch
I saw Harlequin marching to the Curzon Line
    Raise your head high in the light love
And his name was the Red Army
    Open your eyes and cry
I saw Harlequin waltzing in the cornfields
    Lay your head low on my arm love
And his name was the true people
    Close your eyes and dream
            1943

1944. In January, Jennings moved into 8 Regents Park Terrace, Camden Town, the house of Allen Hutt who had introduced him to the Welsh miners during the filming of **Silent Village**. On and off, this was to be his home for the next six years. During March he was seconded from the Crown Film Unit to Two Cities, an independent production company, to do a treatment and script for a film about London and New York. This secondment lasted until May but failed to result in a film. In July he was filming on location in the South of England on a film about the new flying bomb, the V1, the first flying bomb having dropped on London in mid-June. In the autumn he began location work on **A Diary for Timothy**, a film about Britain in what were by now clearly the last months of the war in Europe, and a reflection of how life would be in post-war years. His family returned from America in November 1944.

'Two Cities'

There is a subject for a film to be made by Two Cities which, to my surprise, seems to have escaped everybody, a film of the two cities themselves — London and New York — living simultaneously through twenty-four hours.

There have been quite a number of films made about the life of a single city. They have usually been vivid, symphonic or generalised studies, but there is no doubt that it was found difficult to get drama into them without bringing in a story in an unnatural way. But to make a film about two cities and give each of these cities its representative (its ambassador, so to speak) in the other one, and any human story that you like to play around each of these characters will appear perfectly natural.[. . .]

It would be a picture of propaganda for humanity. Remember that we love people not only for their likeness to us but also for their differences.[. . .]

Do not mistake this paper. What I have suggested here is an idea only, with suggestions for background for the story. A month's work with an American writer will bring to the foreground the four main characters and their adventures. These however must be related to the background and grow out of everyday life. People have often asked for the fusion of the realistic school of film-making with the fictional. Here it is. A small group of actors in the foreground and the vast double canvas of the two great cities beyond them.

Idea for an Anglo-American film 'Two Cities' / 13 January 1944

Jennings rehearsing Myra Hess in
Diary for Timothy

London 1944

The invasion was I think taken here with 'customary British phlegm' . . . but I must say the BBC seems to be doing a first class job. As for the Jerries — either the All-Highest has something very special under his trenchcoat or they just can't make it . . . have been working hard at my book and also a little painting . . . it has become clearer (the painting I mean) less tricky I think but not yet being 40 I suppose I can't be considered to have begun. . .[. . .] The Academy [Cinema] is open again (after being Blitzed early on) and runs excellent old-type programmes — such as *Les Bas Fonds (Jean Gabin)* and *Kline's Forgotten Village* . . . the mind turns more and more I think to the old simple cinema we loved together.

Letter to Cicely Jennings / 9 June 1944

Bedford Square, 5 July 1944

As the syrens were sounding
The children were singing
'Run along little Tishy run along'
As the syrens were sounding
The eyes were brimming
And by the Square railings
A woman was walking
In black cloak and black bonnet
And black scarf waving
As the syrens were sounding
As the eyes were brimming
And the children laughing
'Run along little Tishy run along'

Notes for 'Diary for Timothy'

Dark waves fill the screen: the sea before dawn —
On the wall the BBC signal light flashes
The face of Frederick Allen turns to the microphone: 'Good morning everybody — this is the seven o'clock news for Sunday September 3rd read by Frederick Allen — The fifth anniversary of our entry into the war sees the Germans retreating in the South, the East and the West. . .'
Big Ben in silhouette
The first flare of the sun on the Thames
The shining face of the Sphinx in the Embankment listening also as Allen's voice continues —
Now the voice spreads out over the country this bright September morning
— along trim little streets
— among V1 wreckage

Diary for Timothy (production still)

— out across the fen levels where the wind ruffles the water, past the cathedral towers, the turning windmill
the new pumping station
to be drowned by the roar of Forts and Lancasters wheeling overhead.

As people are going to church the hands of Big Ben touch eleven o'clock — the exact anniversary hour.
Do you remember that same moment — from the same Big Ben — on Sunday September 3rd 1939: 'I am speaking to you from No 10 Downing Street . . . this country is at war with Germany . . . for it is evil things we are fighting against . . . but in the end I am certain the right will prevail . . .'
and today challenging the tired voice from the past comes the wail of the new-born babe — as the camera swings across the row of cots to the pillow of TIMOTHY JAMES JENKINS, the hero of our picture, born today September 3rd, 1944.

39

Diary for Timothy (production still)

On her pillow Tim's mother lies dreaming. Father an RAMC sergeant out in West Africa.

Tim opens his eyes and thinks — of the work & worry, of the grandeur & beauty of the world he knows as yet nothing —
Of the roar of town traffic and the clamour of country markets — nothing —
Of that good soul filling her buckets at the pump and that farmer fretting over his harvest — nothing
Nothing of history either:
>Of the American invasion of Britain
>Of that convoy leaving for the Far East
>Of the newsreels of the liberation of Paris
>Of the latest Hamlet questioning the First Gravedigger:
>'Why was he sent to England?' 'Why because he was mad. . .'
>Of the milk-bar rumours of V2: 'Tom says it's a kind of
>flying refrigerator — come down and freeze everybody. . .'
>Of all this, nothing.
He has never tasted the blackout or seen the Londoners sheltering from V1 in the Tubes.

But all this is the world which he inherits: whose people — whether they know it or not — are working for him — helpless as he lies in the cot:
>the airman, peering through the perspex windscreen
>the engine driver leaning out of his cab
>the farmer looking over the years accounts
>the actor holding up Yorick's skull: 'I knew him, Horatio . . .
>a fellow of infinite jest. . .'
>The miner combing the coal dust out of his hair.

Tim will have his individual place in the world, as they have. What is it to be?

Notebook on **'Diary for Timothy'**/1944

40

1945. Jennings worked on **A Diary for Timothy** until about April. Germany fell in May and he was asked to go to Germany to make a film about life there after defeat and the work of the Military Government. He was on location mainly in Hamburg during September and October.

Germany 1945 / 'A Defeated People'

At lunchtime today we were photographing a family cooking their lunch on campfires in dixies on the blitzed main stair-case of the Palace of Justice at Cologne — one of the few buildings still standing in the centre of the city — outside apparently deserted — surrounded by miles of rubble and weed-covered craters — but inside voices cries of children and the smell of drifting wood-smoke — of burnt paper — the sound of people smashing up doors and windows to light fires in the corridors — the smoke itself drifting into side rooms still littered with legal documents — finally adding to the blue haze in front of the cathedral. The cathedral now with all the damage round immensely tall — a vast blue and unsafe spirit ready to crumble upon the tiny black figures in the street below — permanent figures: Cologne's Black Market. . .and then returning to Düsseldorf — much less knocked about — blitzed but not actually destroyed like Cologne and Essen and Aachen — still a beautiful city, returning here to tea we meeting sailing through the park-like streets a mass of white-Sunday-frocked German school children standing tightly together on an Army truck and singing at the tops of their voices as they are rushed through the streets (where?) . . . In Essen they still fetch their water from stand-pipes and firehose in the streets and the sewers rush roaring and stinking open to the eye and the nose — seep into blitzed houses into cellars where people still live. Look down a deserted street which has a winding path only trodden in the rubble — above the shapes of windows and balconies lean and threaten — below by the front-door now choked with bricks you will see scrawled in chalk 'IM KELLER WOHNEN: . . .' and the names of the families who have taken over the underground passages where there is no light (or once I saw one bulb crawling with bees — they too must live through this winter in Essen) no water — no gas — a ray of daylight from the pavement level airhole.[. . .]

Once no doubt Germany was a beautiful country and still remembers it on summer evenings in the country. For the people themselves they are willing enough or servile enough or friendly enough according to your philosophy of History and the German problem. They certainly don't behave guilty or beaten. They have their old fatalism to fall back on: 'Kaput' says the housewife finding the street water pipe not working. . . and then looks down the street and says 'Kaput . . . alles ist kaput.' Everything's smashed . . . how right — but absoutely no suggestion that it might be their fault — her fault. 'Why' asks another woman fetching water 'why do not you help us?' 'You' being us. At the same time nothing is clearer straight away than that we cannot — must not leave them to stew in their own juice . . . well anyway it's a hell of a tangle.

Letter to Cicely Jennings / 10 September 1945 / Düsseldorf

Post-War:
'The Cumberland Story'/Burma/England/LSO Film Festival of Britain/Death

1946. From March onwards Jennings was working on location in Workington, Cumberland on a film about the modernisation of the mining industry, which was completed as **The Cumberland Story** by early autumn. By the end of the year, he was working with Ian Dalrymple, who had started up his own production company, Wessex Films. They had a project to film *Roaring Century*, a book by R.J.Cruikshank about the century 1846-1946 — which would have fitted in well with Jennings's work on the Industrial Revolution in the unpublished *Pandaemonium*. Money was not forthcoming however.

The Cumberland Story (production still)

Colorado Claro: Thoughts on the 'Cleaned Pictures'

As you approach the rooms containing the 'Cleaned Pictures', between the National Gallery entrance and the rooms themselves you mount a flight of steps flanked by two balconies or wings, on whose walls are hung six pictures which are not really part of the exhibition, but are connected with it: two Renoirs (*Les Parapluies* and *La Première Sortie*), a Manet (*La Servante de Bocks*) a Van Gogh landscape, a Degas oil of an intense brick-orange-red, and a large Delacroix. The choice and placing of these paintings is adroit, to say the least of it. Five of them represent a moment in European painting when the artist's passion for life — for the life around him and for his own craft — had a directness of vision and of method singularly unencumbered by official or theoretical trappings, religious, mythological, political or of his own making. So while these pictures are placed like trumpeters to herald the exhibition, they have also a very practical use in leading our vision from the grey and nervous landscape of Trafalgar Square to the earlier Bacchanalia of Rubens and Poussin.

More than that. Renoir and the rest have not been misted over either by the dirt of Time or by man's 'Gallery varnish' and they are still close enough to us not have become 'sacred'. In front of them a painter still thinks, sees *how* they were painted. [. . .] Among the crowds at the Exhibition (and there are crowds) there are of course those who with a fanatical look in the eye point to the two Velasquez portraits of Philip IV and cry out aloud: 'Velasquez never painted. . .' Of course

1947. In February Jennings went to Burma with a small unit to look at the possibility of making a film of H.E.Bates's book *The Purple Plain*, and he remained there until the beginning of June. His contract with Wessex was renewed and it looks as though it was at this point he worked on a treatment for a film of Thomas Hardy's *Far From the Madding Crowd* for Wessex. He was particularly excited by an exhibition of cleaned pictures at the National Gallery and reviewed it for *Our Time*, where he described his politics as 'those of William Cobbett'.

Drawing / ['Tea Lady', c.1947] / JD69

Painting / ['Tea Lady', c.1947] / JD56

they don't really mean that they were looking over the artist's shoulder in Madrid three centuries ago, though it sounds like it. They mean that the *idea* — the *myth* if you like — of Velasquez on which they have been brought up and nourished, and to which maybe their own painting is related, has been attacked and seriously damaged. They are men defending vested interests. Of course many *ideas* are damaged by this exhibition. The idea for example of Rubens and Claude as painters of *golden* landscapes. The colour of Poussin, even of Veronese (whose work seems most of all to gain from 'cleaning') are seen to be as *bright* (to leave aside for the moment subtler questions) as that of Degas and Renoir. Vollard has reported Renoir's visit to the tobacconist's where he noticed the words *Colorado Claro* on a box of cigars, and saw in them (or in his mistranslation of them) the slogan of his ideal in painting: *Coloré Clair* . . . That is precisely one's impression of the 'Cleaned Pictures'.

The majority of the Old Masters themselves can have had little idea of the use to which their pictures are put to-day, clean or dirty. Little idea of the smoke-trailing city, the island of machines, the atom-haunted world from whose walls their children now look out. The essential thing about the cleaning is that we have now removed the things they did *not* intend — dirt, yellow varnish, and glass . . . the cleaners of the National Gallery under enlightened direction have cleared away so much fake mystery, we must say also that what they have revealed is a thousand times more marvellous, more poetic, and in another sense mysterious [. . .] We can watch Poussin's brush decorate with blue leaf-strokes the white porcelain bowl as it catches the juice of the grape. Leaf-strokes like those with which the girls in the potteries decorate export china. . . and then, not like. The more we gaze (as now we may) — the deeper we look — the more the 'mystery of the craft' affects us. Paint and not paint, simultaneously. Decoration — *coloré, clair* . . . but containing like a signature the character, the emotions, the wishes and regrets of a human lifetime.

Review in *Our Time* / December 1947

The English

[. . .] There are other characteristics of the English, well known to their neighbours, but altogether unmentioned by themselves. Their propensity for endless aggressive war, for example. The Hundred Years War looks quite different from the French side of the Channel. Let those who think it simply a piece of medieval romanticism ask the Scots — or the Welsh — about their experiences. It would be inadvisable to ask the Irish.

[. . .] Now for some strange reason, the Englishman likes to think of himself as a sheep; amd so great is his artistry, so thoroughly does he see himself in any part which he has assumed, that he frequently deceives not only himself, but others. This mild, beneficent creature, easily imposed upon, unmindful of injury, is a pose. But like all the best poses, it takes in its author as well. The English are not hypocritical. They are sincere. In that lies their deadly danger to others.

* * *

The English are in fact a violent, savage race; passionately artistic, enormously addicted to pattern, with a faculty beyond all other people of ignoring their neighbours, their surroundings, or in the last resort, themselves. They have a power of poetry which is the despair of the rest of the world. They produce from time to time personalities transcending ordinary human limitations. Then they drive other nations to a frenzy by patronizing these archangels who have come among them, and by indicating that any ordinary Englishman could do better if he liked to take the trouble. As exemplified in Ben Johnson's insufferable appreciation of Shakespeare.

[. . .] they are hard pressed just now. The English have been a Great Power for quite a long time, and the adjustments necessary if they are to remain in that class are profound. They will require to people continents from their loins, as they did after the discovery of America; but at the same time they will have to recreate the Anglo-French State of the Angevins, and add to it the conquests of Charlemagne. This is an extensive programme. It is certainly worthwhile for them to take stock. What sort of people are they, the oldest of the Old Powers, the youngest — indeed the unborn — of the Newest Powers, starting to challenge Fate again?

43

[. . .] The furious industrial epoch, of which England was the pioneer and of which she is still much the most extreme example, cannot be so put aside. There is no country so urbanized as England. There is no country with so small a percentage of its population engaged on the land. There is no country with such an energy of horse-power heaped and crammed into so small a space. In spite of the fact that a grocer's calender will carry a picture of a cottage in the snow, or that the frontispiece of the *Listener* may show a village spire, England, Modern England, is a series of city streets. The streets of London are paralleled by the streets of Birmingham, by the streets of Yorkshire and Lancashire. Nine out of every ten Englishmen anywhere are born in the towns and bred in the streets.[. . .]

This is the English love of pattern, of order, one of their fundamental qualities. It is responsible for their delight in ships, the supreme example of a patterned life, for their fame abroad as troupe dancers (les Girls), for the spectacle of Trooping the Colour.

[. . .] This absorption in pattern is one aspect of the general power of absorption, of concentration, which the Englishman so specially enjoys. It is possible that this has enabled him to pass into a civilization of streets without becoming a part of it. So the English travel in trains; not a company, but a collection of individuals; first turning each carriage into a row of cottages — the word compartment is a word of praise — and then sitting in each corner with the same blank denial of any other presence that the lovers show in parks. The English live in cities but they are not citified; they seldom produce for example, that characteristic of a city, the mob. They are urbane without being urban; creating their own environment within their own being, they can dwell in the midst of twenty miles of paving stones and pretend, with the aid of a back green or a flower pot, that they are in a hamlet on the Downs. Or so it seems to the outsider. Perhaps the English have something completely different in their heads.

Review of *The English* by Ernest Barker / *Times Literary Supplement* / 7 August 1948

Family Portrait (production stills by H.Usill)

44

A Visit to the Shan States, Burma

We had gone straight north from Rangoon by car along flat country — straight road and paddy-fields for nearly three hundred miles and then began to climb a little into wild cactus country — like pictures of Mexico — the road terrible and stories of dacoits — spent the night at Meiktila — in front of a wonderful lake with splendid pagodas and then the next morning turned east off the main road and made for a hill station called Taunggye which is five thousand feet up and where the mountains and waterfalls and bamboo groves and fir trees really look exactly like Chinese paintings. The people don't speak Burmese and some of the hill tribes wear extraordinary black and dark blue costumes — women in black tunics and trousers with silver ornaments and great black turbans. Splendid Chinese cooking here in the restaurants and (as it is quite cold at night) wood fires — a kind of farm house existence on a permanently perfect day in the Lakes. A few white clouds on the hill tops — a gigantic Buddha protected from the monsoon by roofs of corrugated iron — then Inle lake where the waterside dwellers propel their canoes with one leg round the paddle: called 'leg rowers'. Miles and miles of blue and purple hills, the earth orange or deep red, the bamboos delicate yellows and greens. Returning we came over a private road in the mountains in the country of the Red Karens, who are really wild looking people — animists, not Buddhist — cutting timber and burning patches of the jungle to grow hill-rice. This perilous mountain road brought us at last to Mauchi-mine — which is one of the principal tungsten or wolfram mines in the world. Approached only by two private roads, through jungle and forest — 95 miles to the nearest town — you have to pass armed police at barriers to get in to what is a complete 'lost world'. In a circle of hills there are a mass of bungalows — some belonging to the original Karens who won't work in the mine, some to a complete Sikh and Hindu community who are the miners — and the ones on the top to the Managers and Engineers who are British and South African who have a complete high-class suburban life, with wives and daughters who play tennis and put on long dresses in the evening and grow sweet peas. The company appears to have no allegiance to anyone except Queen Victoria in person who came to an agreement with the Karens. We spent two nights there — going underground (into the side of a hill) to look at the mine — being saluted by the Sikhs at every turn — (but not by the Karens) and then doing the 95 miles back to relative civilisation or barbarism or whatever. Burma is certainly a surprising place.

Letter to Cicely Jennings / 1 March 1947

The London Symphony Orchestra at Work

Saturday, January 8, 1949. Albert Hall.
      Rehearsal with soloists only of *Messiah* under Sir Malcolm Sargent.
      10.30 a.m. Splendid opening picture — a totally empty Albert Hall. We are looking from the steps up from the band room; we can see the lights in the battens and beyond them, in the gloom, 5000 vacant seats. In the foreground the desks are in position but the platform is also bare except for the aged figure of the librarian, who is slowly distributing the orchestral parts, section by

section (the librarian and Ernie the LSO porter are, of course, key figures in the early stages of a rehearsal or concert).

The orchestra assemble (afternoon performance — they are dressed already): two violins, coming as usual from their camping-ground in block H, discuss 'what that flower is', pointing with bow to flower — border along platform edge — similar gesture to that of a player pointing with bow to note in score. As this is a choral work the orchestra are nearly all ranged on the flat; men are straightening seats as usual — soloists enter — slight applause — Sargent enters.

'May I wish you a happy and successful New Year!' — applause. '8', i.e. 8 in a bar — and straight into overture, taking short sections only — opening, sections in middle, and letter F to end.

The two women soloists (Isobel Baillie and Kathleen Ferrier) are sitting muffled up in really arctic-looking furs.

Fragments of each section: 2 — opening leading to 'Comfort ye' — break off — then on to four bars before C (soloist singing sitting), and so on. Opening of 5 — opening of 6. The 'two in bar' section, i.e. 6D prestissimo — then line before I, i.e. the end of 6 and so on; 'that's it — not really *ritardando* — should be *deliberamente*'.

'All right, now we start No 11'; 'beginning of 12'; 13: 'now may I remind you that you do not put on your mutes 2 bars before 8 but 1 bar. . .'

Men in the roof swinging and raising lights: 'In 10 I want special attention to double-basses.'

During the Pastoral Symphony, men in the roof shout 'Wo!' '2 bars before B' — 'Wo' 'Ti-ya- da- ti-ya da. Wait for it, there's no hurry.' S. in his element in Handel. 'You don't listen — I want the outside players to put on their mutes and start playing one bar before B, the inside players stop playing one bar before B — keep the violins up — then you all come in — during 14 you quietly take off your mutes.'

The soloists just indicate their parts — sitting like monks. Roof: 'Up on that one, Harry!' Soprano singing angel's recitative without music in 15. 'Up, Harry! Wo!' '17, please.' '2 bars from the end — really have a short bow at the end then it doesn't go on.' 'Good.' 18: In the gloom under the dome the unlit lamps swing and clank. 'UP!' Imagine the LSO seen from the point of view of Harry in the roof! '21 is out' — everyone marks this.

. . . So on — 'You don't stand for Hallelujah Chorus' — this to orchestra, of course. Discussion of introduction to 45, 'I know that my Redeemer': 'Normal playing — there — everyone can hear the difference — I assure you it's very seldom heard played well — you play exactly what's there — 1.2.3.4. — 1 — 1.2.3.4 — 1'. 48: Discussion of where George Eskdale shall stand for 'The trumpet shall sound'. The string sections in the Amen: 'Strings, that's the real sort of music — it's a joy to hear it clear like that.' Instructions to drummer for end.

The whole of the above rehearsal took one hour and showed what a prodigious stage-manager Sargent is.

'Working Sketches of an Orchestra' / in *London Symphony: Portrait of an Orchestra* / London 1954

45

1948. Until July he was directing **Dim Little Island**, a film with Osbert Lancaster, James Fisher, Ralph Vaughan Williams and an industrialist, John Ormston, about post-war Britain. At the end of the year he had begun work on a possible film about the London Symphony Orchestra at work.

1949. Work on the LSO film continued to the middle of the summer, when he was commissioned by John Grierson and the Festival of Britain Committee to do a film on British achievement for the Festival in 1951. He began work on what was to be **Family Portrait** in August and this continues through to June or July of 1950.

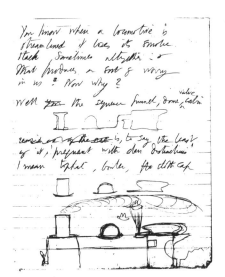

Apples / ['Imaginary Portrait of Sir
Isaac Newton'] / (1940) / MLJ

1950. At the completion of **Family
Portrait** he was asked by the European
Economic Commission to do a film as part
of a series on *The Changing Face of
Europe*. He chose health, and the
projected film was to be *The Good Life*.
He left England at the beginning of
September, looking at possible locations
in France. Switzerland, Italy and then
Greece. He died on the Greek island of
Poros on 24 September, after an accident
in which he slipped and fell from a rock.
He is buried in Athens.

Beware of Locomotives

Driving in a car near Johnson's Wharf and by the railway we came across the notice
'Beware of Locomotives'. We were in a car. It was like the picture by Stubbs of a
cave and in the entrance a white horse who is surprised by a lioness. The horse has
its eyes open with fright and its back legs beginning to give way. The car is the
lioness and the horse the locomotive. There is a well-known type of picture in early
films of a level crossing with an open car and an approaching train with the
terrified eyes of the people in the car, their hands lifted up as the train smashes the
gates. This is a kind of reversal of the horse-lion situation. The horse has become
stronger than the lion. So — Beware of Locomotives.

A steam locomotive is a thing in itself as separate from its train of
trucks or carriages as a horse is from its cart. The transformation of the horse into a
locomotive is perfectly shown in 'The Cyclopede' and in other horse-locomotives
where the horse, from pulling the truck was put inside one with a moving floor
turning the wheels. The transformation of the lions and tigers also into machines
you can find in Blake.

You know when a locomotive is streamlined it loses its smoke stack,
sometimes altogether: and that produces a sort of worry in us. The sequence funnel,
dome, valve and cabin, turns into a class-series: top-hat, Bowler, cloth cap.

Images

It is essential to observe that this selection and presentation of images does not
depend in any way on — the images in this list are not chosen on any power of —
symbolism. They may or may not have been used as symbols of this and that in the
past but at the present they are simple images. A horse is a horse, an apple is an
apple. An image of a horse is an image of a horse, and an image of an apple is an
image of an apple. An image of a horse is an image of a locomotive, an image of an
apple is an image of the sun and so on.

But they are not images of God, or divine Wisdom. Nor are they
significant forms or 'pure forms': an apple is an apple. An object cannot
immediately exchange its being with another object. An apple cannot immediately
become a coal. But an *image* of an object is immediately exchangeable with another
image. An image of a horse can become an image of a locomotive. How?

Precisely through poetry and painting — 'La terre est bleue comme
une orange'.

Beyond the Life of Man / unpublished n.d.

Charles Madge:
A Note on Images

From a pamphlet produced by the Institute of Contemporary Arts,
"Humphrey Jennings, 1907-1950" n.d.[1951]

I think it may help to understand Humphrey Jennings' paintings if one reconsiders what he meant by 'the image'. It was a meaning personal to himself and bound up with his early researches into poetry and painting. His use of 'image' is not far off from the way it is used in psychology, in literary criticism and in surrealist theory, but it is not quite identical with any of these. It has resemblances to the psychological concept of the *gestalt*: 'the combination of many effects, each utterly insensible alone, into one sum of fine effect'.

*'When we admire the sunset we are using the eyes of Turner, when we switch on the light we are tapping the mind of Faraday'. That is a sentence from the script of **Family Portrait**.

The above quotation is not from a *gestalt* psychologist, but from the *Diary* of Michael Faraday, the physicist,* and is part of a passage, dated June 1850, which is included by Humphrey Jennings in *Pandaemonium*, his great collection of 'images' chosen to illustrate the transformation in our way of looking at the world between 1660 and 1866. The full passage from Faraday's diary is as follows and constitutes in itself a kind of 'image of the image':

'A balloon went up on Saturday Evng. (22 instant) from Vauxhall. The evening was very clear and the Sun bright: the balloon was very high, so that I could not see the car from Queen Square, Bloomsbury, and looked like a golden ball. Ballast was thrown out two or three times and was probably sand; but the dust of it had this effect, that a stream of golden cloud seemed to descend from the balloon, shooting downwards for a moment, and then remained apparently stationary, the balloon and it separating very slowly. It shews the wonderful manner in which (each) particle of this dusty cloud must have made its impression on the eye by the light reflected from it, and is a fine illustration of the combination of many effects, each utterly insensible alone, into one sum of fine effect'.

Locomotive / [c.1936] / JD74

The 'image' here consists not only of the balloon, the golden cloud of dust particles, Vauxhall, the date, Faraday watching and Faraday's physical discoveries, but of the relations between these elements and other elements, all ordered into a larger universe of imagery. The individual image, and the imaginative eye that seizes it, is a point of *ordonnance* in such a universe. It is not only verbal, or visual, or emotional, although it is all these. It is not in the elements, but in their coming together at a particular moment, that the magical potency lies.

'But at the present moment the Surrealists (especially Ernst) are exploiting the rather temporary emotive qualities of incongruity provided by the juxtaposition of objects as objects (with literary associations). There are other pieces of myth-construction in *la jeune peinture*, related to Surrealism: dream-suggestion has been used by Sima, metamorphosis and animal combats by Masson, and Roux has extended the idea of metamorphosis into a complete world-reconstruction by symbolism. The work of these painters also relies greatly on the actual shock of following the literary metamorphosis. Thus, both technique and myth are at present using our associations for their power; a state of affairs which by its nature cannot last. A new solidity as firm as Cubism, but fluid, not static, is required. Precisely such a solidity both of technique and myth we find in South African rock painting...'

This is one of Humphrey Jennings's very few published statements on painting. It comes from an essay on 'Rock-painting and *La jeune peinture*', signed by himself and G.F.Noxon, which appeared in the Spring number of *Experiment* (a Cambridge magazine) in 1931, twenty years ago. It explains very well what he aimed at in his own painting. 'A new solidity as firm as Cubism, but fluid'. The art that Humphrey Jennings was seeking must reflect a cosmos in flux. In this flux are assemblages, or shapes, or patterns, of relative intensity, and fixity, and certainty. Paradoxically solid and fluid, the images are moments in the flow of human experience. The shape is solid, but the line that encloses it is fluid, as it awaits the next metamorphosis.

In the same essay, Jennings calls for 'the use of technique, to create mutations in the subject, and the subject thereby to be in its proper place, as the basis of a metamorphosis by paint and not by literary substitution'. *Metamorphosis by paint* is in three words what Humphrey Jennings attempted as a painter and he took his medium seriously. In this medium, the canvas and the paint mattered; in poetry, the voice and the page. Both poetry and painting, as he understood them, are outside 'literature', or more strictly are on planes intersecting the literary plane. Jennings in conversation often asserted his independence of literature, which he saw as a muddle of unrealised images and inadequate techniques. His aim was to seize and create 'mutations in the subject', liberating human perceptions from the literature that surrounds them.

The 'subject' of a painting, or a poem, is therefore the nucleus of an image, the ordering point. Humphrey Jennings returned again and again to certain 'subjects', in his battle to transform them. The horse, the steam engine, the plough, the dome of St.Paul's, these were some of his 'subjects' and they are the nucleus or core of images that he created in paint, in poetry and in film.

The image of the plough, to take an example, is illustrated in some of the paintings in this exhibition. The same image appears in a poem, 'The Plough', written in 1948:

The gallows, the vine, the gang, the beet, the subsoil, the hoe,
The Norfolk wheel,
Whether in Tull's tune-book, Jefferson's design, on the Illinois prairie or
                    pagoda ground,
All, all I see reflected in the giant shadow plough;
The gallows coloured green, the vine coloured red, the gang-plough
                    lemon yellow, sombre purples and browns,
And the Norfolk wheel itself deep blue, standing alone in the snow.

These names 'the gallows, the vine' and so on, are kinds of plough. Jethro Tull was a musician and designer of ploughs in the early eighteenth century. Jefferson is Thomas Jefferson, third president of the United States, and also a designer of ploughs. There are references to America and the Far East, but the emphatic reference is to Jennings's native East Anglia. The image therefore has

*John Rickman: 'The Development of Psychological Medicine', *British Medical Journal*, 7 January 1950 'Whether that inner labour results in anything which is socially applauded or has social uses varies with each individual. But, useful or not socially, it is a source of gratification to the individual it gives, if it is in low degree, that meed of pleasure without which mental life of human standard seems not to operate; when in high degree, it gives that rare sweeping ''oceanic'' exultation of spirit and creative ecstasy which the artists, of all men, can best communicate to their fellows'.

historical and geographical coordinates but it belongs also to that 'inner labour', that 'private zone of culture', which the psycho-analyst * finds to be characteristic of 'the artist and scientist, the mystic and the lunatic — for that matter all of us' and on which we expend so much of our mental energies. In the poem on the plough, and by implication in the paintings, there is a distinction between the local, coloured ploughs and the achromatic, abstracted 'giant shadow plough', in its primitive simplicity, a 'giant' because 'culture' itself means, literally, tillage. Yet in another sense the colours represent the poetry of the plough, as opposed to its utility. Or rather, it is by those to whom the plough is coloured by poetry that new kinds of plough will be designed. (Jethro Tull designed his ploughs on analogies suggested by musical instruments.) In this sense, Humphrey Jennings is attempting a *metamorphosis of the plough by paint*: and not of the plough only, but by implication a metamorphosis of other 'means of production', to use the Marxist phrase.

49

Another example will further illustrate how an image has both a local and a universal significance. In one of his 'war poems' Jennings wrote:

I see London.
I see the dome of Saint Paul's like the forehead of Darwin.

The image of St. Paul's and its dome is recurrent also in those paintings in which is depicted a kind of generalised landscape of London. In *Pandaemonium*, many passages centre around St. Paul's. In particular there is a very beautiful quotation from Faraday in which, by an optical illusion, it seemed that 'rays of darkness were issuing from the Church' — a radar-like image. St. Paul's embodies in its architecture the rational side of protestantism. It stands as a monument to the opening of that great epoch of material and mental transformation with which *Pandaemonium* is concerned. And yet at the same time the dome of St. Paul's is only one dome of many domes. It stands for all the domes and, by metaphor, for all the dome-like foreheads of scientists, for the collective intellection of centuries and nations.

St. Paul's is magnificently photographed in **Family Portrait**, Humphrey Jennings's last film in which he tried to put our past, present and future in simple but persuasive unity. His understanding of the past, his sense of the present, were vivified by his acceptance of the future. To quote from the script of **Family Portrait** which he wrote so soon before his death:

'Tonight there are new shapes on the skylines of home . . . the fantastic antennae of modern science, reaching out to the unknown . . . Peacetime versions of radar picking up radio waves coming in from the blank spaces in the Milky Way — or plotting the tracks of meteors as they rush through the sky . . .'
'That's a meteor there . . .'
Some of the more recent paintings have short lines flying through them which suggest the tracks of meteors, or the paths of atomic particles, and these paintings undoubtedly are connected with the imaginative impact of modern physics. They record something of the meteoric quality of Humphrey Jennings himself.

St. Paul's Cathedral / (1942) / JD35

Kathleen Raine:
Humphrey Jennings
From the ICA pamphlet [1951]

Those who knew Humphrey Jennings took his genius for granted, as we do the sun. Natural phenomena cause no surprise; and Humphrey's mind had the quality of Tao (not that he would have called himself a taoist, if only because 'the names that can be named are not the universal names'), the apparent simplicity of light, or the solar system. Only now that he is removed, we are aware that we shall never again know anything like it. His greatness, like that of Coleridge, is something that only those who knew him can fully realise; for it was the total phenomenon of his remarkable mind, activated by the most powerful imagination I have ever encountered in a living man, that made knowing him such a wonderful experience to those who came within measuring distance of understanding him.

How much of that genius is expressed in his paintings will be judged finally by those who never knew him. He always regarded himself as, before everything, a painter; film-making was of secondary importance and the writing of poems an occasional mode of expression; and it is significant that Humphrey himself said, early last year, that he had just begun to be sufficiently satisfied with his work to feel that the time had come for an exhibition. He had mastered his style.

Humphrey was aware of most of his problems twenty years ago; but those who listened, spellbound by his discourses on his theories of painting, would have been baffled by the canvases alone. Sometimes he would paint some apparently naively simple, realistic object — like a matchbox; or, approaching the problem from another point of view, only a few brushmarks, of infinite delicacy of touch and subtlety of colour, on canvases left largely bare — so left because every brushmark must be made with meaning, deliberately placed according to a complex imaginative operation, involving both conscious thought and instinctive sensibility. How few poets or painters know even so much of truth as to avoid falsehood. In about the year 1929, Humphrey was preoccupied for months with the problem of where the first brushmark, that determines the whole painting, should be made on the canvas. French in visual perception, English in his sense of the poetic image, Chinese in his philosophy of how an action (painting in particular) should be performed, he sought simultaneously for three kinds of truth; in his mature work, so it seems to me, all these are achieved.

Humphrey Jennings may be seen as a product of the same school (that of Professor I.A.Richards's 'scientific' literary criticism) that produced William Empson's conception of the ambiguity (more properly the multiplicity) of the poetic statement. Charles Madge has said virtually all that need to be said on Humphrey Jennings's idea of the Image, but in parenthesis I may mention one source on which he drew which might be overlooked — the syncretic images of the Tarot. Two of these especially are recurring themes in his paintings — the Chariot, resolving itself into horse-team and locomotive; and the '*maison Dieu*', the house struck by fire from heaven. The latter was one of Humphrey Jennings's key images many years before the war made the symbol actual, and provided him with the theme of his film, **Fires Were Started**; but it was, to his astonishingly objective mind, in the very nature of a symbolic situation that it must produce itself, as an event, in historical actuality. This must follow from the fact that history, as Humphrey Jennings, like Blake, conceived it, is the realisation of human imaginings. In this he went a stage beyond the surrealists, for whom the mental elaboration of images was sufficient in itself; for Humphrey Jennings the final test of an image was its objective reality. Take the Chariot, the abstract Tarot symbol of human power and achievement, one of Humphrey's earliest themes. Gray, in the Progress of Poesy, describes successively the Triumph of Mars, Hyperion, and at last the poet himself, in symbols no less characteristic of Humphrey Jennings than of Gray himself:

> Behold . . . (the poet's) car
> Wide o'er the fields of glory bear
> Two coursers of etherial race
> With necks in thunder clothed, and long-resounding pace.

Analysing the image, Humphrey referred it back to Milton's 'Chariot of paternal deity'; but the image must be realised as well as analysed. In his last film, **Family Portrait**, as the commentator speaks a line of Blake, that, in itself, refers back both to Gray and Milton, 'bring me my chariot of fire', a locomotive moves slowly forwards, symbol of the Triumph of the Iron Horse. History must realise, or it is mere literature.

Certainly no poet, since Blake, has understood English history, and in particular the Industrial Revolution, with the twofold intensity of observation and imagination that Humphrey Jennings brought to bear on the industrial landscape, the locomotive, the fine instruments of modern science. For him, as for Blake, London was 'a human awful wonder of God'. Yet as against the advance of the locomotive, we have the figure of Lord Byron, man born free, who refuses 'the unvarying pace between rocky walls' imposed by the triumph of the machine. It is impossible to say in few words what conclusions Humphrey Jennings had reached on questions of such complexity as those presented by the Industrial Revolution; but it is perhaps significant that it is to the pre-industrial symbols of the Plough, the Windmill, and the Harvest Field that he returned most often, and to the horse, docile yet wild. The culture of the Plough and the Horse reverences and preserves the earth and the natural instincts of the living creature and it was culture of this kind that H.J. found and loved in provincial France, in Burma, and in the villages of Greece. On almost the last occasion that I saw him, we were walking over Battersea Bridge, Humphrey propounding a Utopian scheme for turning the foul waters of

Byron's House at Missolonghi / (1939-40)
A.R.V.Cooper

the Thames into fish-ponds. Raising his arm with a characteristic gesture towards the industrial landscape from Lots Road Power Station to Battersea, he said, 'This has all grown up within less than two hundred years. Has anyone ever suggested that this was the way in which human beings ought to live? It will all have to go, it has been a terrible mistake!' Not that he envisaged a return to any particular period, or any return at all. All his feeling was for the modern, for the growing-point of the living organism of Man society. The symbols that he sought to create or recreate belong neither to past nor future, but to certain permanent principles that must be observed for the preservation of man in a stable and mutually life-giving relationship with the earth that he inhabits, its natural forces and resources.

52

Cornfield / [c.1948] / MLJ

Lindsay Anderson:

Only Connect
Some Aspects of the Work of Humphrey Jennings

Sight and Sound / April-June 1954

It is difficult to write anything but personally about the films of Humphrey Jennings. This is not of course to say that a full and documented account of his work in the cinema would not be of the greatest interest: anyone who undertook such a study would certainly merit our gratitude. But the sources are diffuse. Friends and colleagues would have to be sought out and questioned; poems and paintings tracked down; and, above all, the close texture of the films themselves would have to be exhaustively examined. My aim must be more modest, merely hoping to stimulate by offering some quite personal reactions, and by trying to explain why I think these pictures are so good.

Jennings's films are all documentaries, all made firmly within the framework of the British documentary movement. This fact ought not to strike a chill, for surely 'the creative interpretation of actuality' should suggest an exciting, endlessly intriguing use of the cinema; and yet it must be admitted that the overtones of the term are not immediately attractive. Indeed it comes as something of a surprise to learn that this unique and fascinating artist was from the beginning of his career in films an inside member of Grierson's GPO Unit (with which he first worked in 1934), and made all his best films as official, sponsored propaganda during the second world war. His subjects were thus, at least on the surface, the common ones; yet his manner of expression was always individual, and became more and more so. It was a style that bore the closest possible relationship to his theme — to that aspect of his subjects which his particular vision caused him consistently to stress. It was, that is to say, a poetic style. In fact it might reasonably be contended that Humphrey Jennings is the only real poet the British cinema has yet produced.

II

He started directing films in 1939 (we may leave out of account an insignificant experiment in 1935, in collaboration with Len Lye); and the date is significant, for it was the war that fertilised his talent and created the conditions in which his best work was produced. Watching one of Jennings's early pictures, **Speaking from America,** which was made to explain the workings of the transatlantic radio-telephone system, one would hardly suspect the personal qualities that characterise the pictures he was making only a short while later. There seems to have been more evidence of these in **Spare Time,** a film on the use of leisure among industrial workers: a mordant sequence of a carnival procession, drab and shoddy, in a Northern city aroused the wrath of more orthodox documentarians, and Basil Wright has mentioned other scenes, more sympathetically shot: 'the pigeon-fancier, the ''lurcher-loving collier'' and the choir rehearsal are all important clues to

53

A sequence from
A Diary for Timothy
The characters have been introduced
and the theme of the film established —
a poetic summary of life in Britain
during the last year of the war.
The sequence is set in the late summer
and autumn of 1944. It begins with the
voice of Michael Redgrave reading
E.M.Forster's commentary in voice over.
Shot scale is indicated as follows:
Close-up C.U. / close shot C.S. /
Medium shot M.S. / long shot L.S.

1. 'And you didn't know, and couldn't know; and
didn't care. Safe in your pram'.
A bugle call sounds, faintly.
2. L.S.Quarry. A group of miners some distance
away are looking at a newspaper.
'But listen, Tim; listen to this'.
The call continues.

3. Bugle call swells up.
4. The headline of the newspaper flapping in the
wind: the word ARNHEM.
Bugle call fades under the voice of Frank Phillips
reading a BBC war report
'About five miles to the west of Arnhem. . .'
5. A wireless set. The camera tracks in.
'. . . in a space 1,500 yards by 900 on that last day
I saw the dead and the living. . .'

Humphrey's development'. Certainly such an affectionate response to simple
pleasures is more characteristic of Jennings's later work than any emphasis of satire.

If there had been no war, though, could that development ever have
taken place? Humphrey Jennings was never happy with narrowly propagandist
subjects, any more than he was with the technical exposition of **Speaking from
America.** But in wartime people become important, and observation of them is
regarded in itself as a justifiable subject for filming, without any more specific
'selling angle' than their sturdiness of spirit. Happily, this was the right subject for
Jennings. With Cavalcanti, Harry Watt and Pat Jackson he made **The First Days**,
a picture of life on the home front in the early months of the war. On his own, he then
directed **Spring Offensive**, about farming and the new development of
agricultural land in the Eastern counties; in 1940 he worked again with Harry Watt
on **London Can Take It**, another picture of the home front; and in 1941, with
Heart of Britain, he showed something of the way in which the people of Northern
industrial Britain were meeting the challenge of war.

These films did their jobs well, and social historians of the future will
find in them much that makes vivid the atmosphere and manners of their period.
Ordinary people are sharply glimpsed in them, and the ordinary sounds that were
part of the fabric of their lives reinforce the glimpses and sometimes comment on
them: a lorry-load of youthful conscripts speeds down the road in blessed ignorance
of the future, as a jaunty singer gives out 'We're going to hang out our washing on
the Siegfried line'. In the films which Jennings made in collaboration, it is risky, of
course, to draw attention too certainly to any particular feature as being his: yet
here and there are images and effects which unmistakably betray his sensibility.
Immense women knitting furiously for the troops; a couple of cockney mothers
commenting to each other on the quietness of the streets now that the children have
gone; the King and Queen unostentatiously shown inspecting the air raid damage
in their own back garden. **Spring Offensive** is less sure in its touch, rather
awkward in its staged conversations and rather over-elaborate in its images; **Heart
of Britain** plainly offered a subject that Jennings found more congenial. Again the
sense of human contact is direct: a steel-worker discussing his ARP duty with his
mate, a sturdy matron of the WVS looking straight at us through the camera as she
touchingly describes her pride at being able to help the rescue workers, if only by
serving cups of tea. And along with these plain, spontaneous encounters come
telling shots of landscape and background, amplifying and reinforcing. A style, in
fact, is being hammered out in these films; a style based on a peculiar intimacy of
observation, a fascination with the commonplace thing or person that is significant
precisely because it is commonplace, and with the whole pattern that can emerge
when such commonplace, significant things and people are fitted together in the
right order.

Although it is evident that the imagination at work in all these early
pictures is instinctively a cinematic one, in none of them does one feel that the
imagination is working with absolute freedom. All the films are accompanied by
commentaries, in some cases crudely propagandist, in others serviceable and decent
enough; but almost consistently these off-screen words clog and impede the progress

6. A working class family group gathered round their wireless.
'... those who fought the good fight and kept the faith with you at home, and those who still fought magnificently on. They were the last of the few.'
7. C.U. wireless set speaker.
'I last saw them yesterday morning, as they dribbled into Nijmegen.'

8. 'They had staggered and walked and waded all night from Arnhem, about ten miles north. We were busy asking each other if this or that one had been seen.'
9. C.U. another wireless.
'Late in the afternoon before, we were told that the remnants of the 1st Airborne Division were going to pull out that night.'
10. C.U. Tim's mother listening.
'Perhaps I should remind you here that these were men of no ordinary calibre. They'd been nine days in that little space I mentioned, being mortared and shelled, machine-gunned and sniped from all round.'
11. C.U. another wireless.
'For the last three days they had no water, very little but small arms ammunition, and rations cut to one-sixth.'

12. 'Luckily or unluckily it rained, and they caught the water in their capes and drank that. These last items were never mentioned: they were Airborne weren't they; they were tough and knew it. All right: water and rations didn't matter — give them some Germans to kill, and one chance in ten, and they'd get along somehow.'
At 'water and rations' the sound of Beethoven's Appassionata sonata creeps in softly.

of the picture. The images are so justly chosen, and so explicitly assembled, that there is nothing for the commentator to say. The effect — particularly if we have Jennings's later achievements in mind — is cramped. The material is there, the elements are assembled; but the fusion does not take place that alone can create the poetic whole that is greater than the sum of its parts. And then comes the last sequence of **Heart of Britain.** The Huddersfield Choral Society rises before Malcolm Sargent, and the homely, buxom housewives, the black-coated workers, and the men from the mills burst into the Hallelujah Chorus. The sound of their singing continues, and we see landscapes and noble buildings, and then a factory where bombers are being built. Back and forth go these contrasting, conjunctive images, until the music broadens out to its conclusion, the roar of engines joins in, and the bombers take off. The sequence is not a long one, and there are unfortunate intrusions from the commentator, but the effect is extraordinary, and the implications obvious. Jennings has found his style.

III

Words for Battle, Listen to Britain, Fires Were Started, A Diary for Timothy. To the enthusiast for Jennings these titles have a ring which makes it a pleasure simply to speak them, or to set them down in writing; for these are the films in which, between 1941 and 1945, we can see that completely individual style developing from tentative discovery and experiment to mature certainty. They are all films of Britain at war, and yet their feeling is never, or almost never, warlike. They are committed to the war — for all his sensibility there does not seem to have been anything of the pacifist about Jennings — but their real inspiration is pride, an unaggressive pride in the courage and doggedness of ordinary British people. Kathleen Raine, a friend of Jennings and his contemporary at Cambridge, has written: 'What counted for Humphrey was the expression, by certain people, of the ever-growing spirit of man; and, in particular, of the spirit of England'.
It is easy to see how the atmosphere of the country at war could stimulate and inspire an artist so bent. For it is at such a time that the spirit of a country becomes manifest, the sense of tradition and community sharpened as (alas) it rarely is in time of peace. 'He sought therefore for a public imagery, a public poetry.' In a country at war we are all members one of another, in a sense that is obvious to the least spiritually-minded.
'*Only connect*'. It is surely no coincidence that Jennings chose for his writer on **A Diary for Timothy** the wise and kindly humanist who had placed that epigraph on the title page of his best novel. The phrase at any rate is apt to describe not merely the film on which Jennings worked with E.M.Forster, but this whole series of pictures which he made during the war. He had a mind that delighted in simile and the unexpected relationship. ('It was he', wrote Grierson, 'who discovered the Louis Quinze properties of a Lyons' swiss roll'.) On a deeper level, he loved to link one event with another, the past with the present, person to person. Thus the theme of **Words for Battle** is the interpretation of great poems of the past through events of the present — a somewhat artificial idea, though brilliantly executed. It is perhaps significant, though, that the film springs to a new kind of life

13. Camera tracks back from keyboard.
The Appassionata: forte chords on cut.

14. L.S. Platform at a National Gallery concert.
Myra Hess at piano.
Appassionata continues.

15. Appassionata continues through the rest of this
sequence, to shot 27.

16. Poster announcing Fifth Birthday Concert at the
National Gallery.

17. Camera tracks along a row of listening faces.

18. M.S. Myra Hess at piano. Camera tracks in to
her hands.
Under music BBC commentator's voice is faded up,
repeating:
'. . . Luckily or unluckily it rained, and they caught
the water in their capes and drank that. . .'

altogether in its last sequence, as the words of Lincoln at Gettysburg are followed by the clatter of tanks driving into Parliament Square past the Lincoln statue: the sound of the tanks merges in turn into the grand music of Handel, and suddenly the camera is following a succession of men and women in uniform, striding along the pavement cheery and casual, endowed by the music, by the urgent rhythm of the cutting, and by the solemnity of what has gone before (to which we feel they are heirs) with an astonishing and breathtaking dignity, a mortal splendour.

As if taking its cue from the success of this wonderful passage, **Listen to Britain** dispenses with commentary altogether. Here the subject is simply the sights and sounds of wartime Britain over a period of some twenty-four hours. To people who have not seen the film it is difficult to describe its fascination — something quite apart from its purely nostalgic appeal to anyone who lived through those years in this country. The picture is a stylistic triumph (Jennings shared the credit with his editor, Stewart McAllister), a succession of marvellously evocative images freely linked by contrasting and complementary sounds; and yet it is not for its quality of form that one remembers it most warmly, but for the continuous sensitivity of its human regard. It is a fresh and loving eye that Jennings turns on to those Canadian soldiers, singing to an accordion to while away a long train journey; or on to that jolly factory girl singing 'Yes my Darling Daughter' at her machine; or on to the crowded floor of the Blackpool Tower Ballroom; or the beautiful, sad-faced woman who is singing 'The Ash Grove' at an ambulance station piano. Emotion in fact (it is something one often forgets) can be conveyed as unmistakably through the working of a film camera as by the manipulation of pen or paint brush. To Jennings this was a transfigured landscape, and he recorded its transfiguration on film.

The latter two of these four films, **Fires Were Started** and **A Diary for Timothy**, are more ambitious in conception: the second runs for about forty minutes, and the first is a full-length 'feature-documentary'. One's opinion as to which of them is Jennings's masterpiece is likely to vary according to which of them one has most recently seen. **Fires Were Started** (made in 1943) is a story of one particular unit of the National Fire Service during one particular day and night in the middle of the London blitz: in the morning the men leave their homes and civil occupations, their taxi-cabs, newspaper shops, advertising agencies, to start their tour of duty; a new recruit arrives and is shown the ropes; warning comes in that a heavy attack is expected; night falls and the alarms begin to wail; the unit is called out to action at a riverside warehouse, where fire threatens an ammunition ship drawn up at the wharf; the fire is mastered; a man is lost; the ship sails with the morning tide. In outline it is the simplest of pictures; in treatment it is of the greatest subtlety, richly poetic in feeling, intense with tenderness and admiration for the unassuming heroes whom it honours. Yet is is not merely the members of the unit who are given this depth and dignity of treatment. Somehow every character we see, however briefly, is made to stand out sharply and memorably in his or her own right: the brisk and cheery girl who arrives with the dawn on the site of the fire to serve tea to the men from her mobile canteen; a girl in the control room forced under her desk by a near-miss, and apologising down the telephone which she still holds in her hand as she picks herself up; two isolated aircraft-spotters watching the

19. Sudden forte in music precipitates cut.
20. L.S. Another static water tank in London street.
21. Bombed roofs of London houses.
The voice of Michael Redgrave returns reading
E.M.Forster's commentary, 'It's the middle of
October now . . .'
Appassionata continuing under commentary.
22. A builder mending slates on a bombed roof.
'And the war certainly won't be over by Christmas.
And the weather doesn't suit us. . .'
23. Another roof mender.
'And one-third of all our houses have been damaged
by enemy action.'
The sound of the workman's hammer pierces the
music.

24. 'Did you like the music that lady was playing?
Some of us think it is the greatest music in the world.
Yet it's German music, and we're fighting the Germans.'
At 'some of us think. . .' the pianist's hands are
superimposed over the image of roofmenders.
25. C.U. Pianist's hands.
'There's something you'll have to think over later on.'
26. The wet surface of a road; the legs of a man
leading a pony pass diagonally across frame.
Sound of water trickling merges with Appassionata.
'Rain . . . too much rain.'
27. A miner at the coal face.
'It's even wet under the earth.'
The Appassionata is lost under the sound of picking.

flames of London miles away through the darkness. No other British film made
during the war, documentary or feature, achieved such a continuous and poignant
truthfulness, or treated the subject of men at war with such a sense of its incidental
glories and its essential tragedy.

The idea of connection, by contrast and juxtaposition, is always present
in **Fires Were Started** — never more powerfully than in the beautiful closing
sequence, where the fireman's sad little funeral is intercut against the ammunition
ship moving off down the river — but its general movement necessarily conforms to
the basis of narrative. **A Diary for Timothy**, on the other hand, is constructed
entirely to a pattern of relationships and contrasts, endlessly varying, yet each one
contributing to the rounded poetic statement of the whole. It is a picture of the last
year of the war, as it was lived through by people in Britain; at the start a baby,
Timothy, is born, and it is to him that the film is addressed. Four representative
characters are picked out (if we except Tim himself and his mother, to both of whom
we periodically return): an engine driver, a farmer, a Welsh miner and a wounded
fighter pilot. But the story is by no means restricted to scenes involving these; with
dazzling virtuosity, linking detail to detail by continuously striking associations of
image, sound, music and comment, the film ranges freely over the life of the nation,
connecting and connecting. National tragedies and personal tragedies, individual
happinesses and particular beauties are woven together in a design of the utmost
complexity: the miner is injured in a fall at the coal face, the fighter pilot gets better
and goes back to his unit, the Arnhem strike fails, Myra Hess plays Beethoven at the
National Gallery, bombs fall over Germany, and Tim yawns in his cot.

Such an apparently haphazard selection of details could mean nothing
or everything. Some idea of the poetic method by which Jennings gave the whole
picture its continual sense of emotion and significance may perhaps be given by the
sequence analysed and illustrated here, but of course only the film can really speak
for itself. The difficulty of writing about such a film, of disengaging in the memory
the particular images and sounds (sounds moreover which are constantly
overlapping and mixing with each other) from the overall design has been
remarked on by Dilys Powell:

'It is the general impression which remains; only with an effort do
you separate the part from the whole . . . the communication is always through a
multitude of tiny impressions, none in isolation particularly memorable.'
Only with the last point would one disagree. **A Diary for Timothy** is so tensely
constructed, its progression is so swift and compulsive, its associations and
implications so multifarious, that it is almost impossible, at least for the first few
viewings, to catch and hold on to particular impressions. Yet the impressions
themselves are rarely unmemorable, not merely for their splendid pictorial quality,
but for the intimate and loving observation of people, the devoted concentration on
the gestures and expressions, the details of dress or behaviour that distinguish each
unique human being from another. Not least among the virtues that distinguish
Jennings from almost all British film-makers is his respect for personality, his
freedom from the inhibitions of class-consciousness, his inability to patronise or
merely to use the people in his films. Jennings's people are ends in themselves.

57

28. A miner heaps coal on to a conveyor.
'Look at the place where Goronwy has to cut coal.'
The fierce sound of drilling on the cut.
29. C.S. Drill.
Drilling continues.

30. 'And you — all warm and sleepy in your cot by
the fire...'
The subdued sound of rain trickling down a window
pane.

* **Listen to Britain** was shown on BBC — in 1946

IV

Other films were made by Jennings during the war, and more after it, up to his tragic death in 1950; but I have chosen to concentrate on what I feel to be his best work, most valuable to us. He had his theme, which was Britain; and nothing else could stir him to quite the same response. With more conventional subjects — **The Story of Lili Marlene, A Defeated People, The Cumberland Story** — he was obviously unhappy, and, despite his brilliance at capturing the drama of real life, the staged sequences in these films do not suggest that he would have been at ease in the direction of features. **The Silent Village** — his reconstruction of the story of Lidice in a Welsh mining village — bears this out; for all the fond simplicity with which he sets his scene, the necessary sense of conflict and suffering is missed in his over-refined, under-dramatised treatment of the essential situation. It may be maintained that Jennings's peacetime return to the theme of Britain (**The Dim Little Island** in 1949, and **Family Portrait** in 1950) produced work that can stand beside his wartime achievement, and certainly neither of these two beautifully finished films is to be dismissed. But they lack passion.

By temperament Jennings was an intellectual artist, perhaps too intellectual for the cinema. (It is interesting to find Miss Raine reporting that, 'Julian Trevelyan used to say that Humphrey's intellect was too brilliant for a painter.') It needed the hot blast of war to warm him to passion, to quicken his symbols to emotional as well as intellectual significance. His symbols in **Family Portrait** — the Long Man of Wilmington, Beachy Head, the mythical horse of Newmarket — what do they really mean to us? Exquisitely presented though it is, the England of those films is nearer the 'This England' of the pre-war beer advertisements and Mr Castleton Knight's coronation film than to the murky and undecided realities of today. For reality, his wartime films stand alone; and they are sufficient achievement. They will last because they are true to their time, and because the depth of feeling in them can never fail to communicate itself. They will speak for us to posterity, saying: 'This is what it was like. This is what we were like — the best of us'.

Postscript

October 1981

Since 'Only Connect' was published in *Sight and Sound* in 1954, I have written several times about Humphrey Jennings. One always hopes — without too much presumption — that one is helping to keep the work alive. Yet as the years pass, these films, which should be familiar to every schoolboy and girl in the country, seem to be seen and known by fewer people. As far as I know, BBC Television, which in recent years has shown films like *The Foreman Went to France, Angels One Five, The Way to the Stars* etc., has practically never shown a film by Humphrey Jennings in its entirety.* (They commissioned Robert Vas to make a film about him but the result was, as usual with Robert's films, as much about Robert himself as about Jennings. And the extracts from Jennings's work could surely not mean a great deal to people who were not already familiar with it.) Recently, perched on a camera crane waiting for clouds to pass, I asked the crew how many of them had heard of Humphrey Jennings. One had. But he could not remember the name of any of his films.

So I am happy that Riverside Studios are mounting this exhibition; that this book is being prepared; and that 'Only Connect' has been chosen for reprinting. Although it was written nearly thirty years ago, it still reflects pretty faithfully what I feel. I got into trouble when it was first published, for saying that Jennings was 'the only real poet the British cinema has yet produced'. Lady Elton was particularly annoyed — though, with the exception of Basil Wright, I cannot see that the British documentary movement produced any other director who could be called a poet. But then (again with the exception of Basil) I don't think the British documentarists ever really approved of Jennings; certainly they never expressed any enthusiasm for his work until it was too late. The Griersonian tradition — into which Jennings only fitted uneasily — was always more preachy and sociological than it was either political or poetic.

One aspect of Humphrey Jennings's work I would have to be stricter about if I were writing today: its last phase. My allusion in this piece to **Dim Little Island** and **Family Portrait** is pussy-footing and unilluminating. Of course there is distinctive and distinguished compositional style to these films. But in the end they *can* be dismissed. In fact they must be. They demonstrate only too sadly how the traditionalist spirit was unable to adjust itself to the changed circumstances of Britain after the war. By the time Jennings made **Family Portrait** for the 1951 Festival of Britain, the 'family' could only be a sentimental fiction, inhabiting a Britain dedicated to the status quo. I don't know whether Jennings thought of himself as a 'Leftist' in the old Mass Observation days. Traditionalism, after all, does not always have to be equated with Conservatism. But somehow by the end of the war, Jennings's traditionalism had lost any touch of the radical: **Spare Time** (which is a beautiful, sharp, bitter-sweet and touching picture) is infinitely more alive than his academic **Family Portrait.** He found himself invoking great names of the past (Darwin, Newton, Faraday and Watt) in an attempt to exorcise the demons of the present. Even the fantasy of Empire persists ('The crack of the village bat is heard on Australian plains. . .'). The symbol at the end of the film is the mace of Authority, and its last image is a preposterous procession of ancient and bewigged dignitaries. The Past is no longer an inspiration: it is a refuge.

But of course whether Humphrey Jennings was able to find the inspiration in peace that he had in war does not matter. That particular problem has been ours rather than his for some time now: and we can hardly claim to have solved it much better. There remain his precious handful of films. They may not seem directly dedicated to our dilemmas; but they can still stir and inspire us with their imaginative and moral impulse, they are still alive (for those who have eyes to see and ears to hear) with that mysterious oracular power which is the magic property of art. The poetry survives.

More than a Shadow:
Humphrey Jennings and Stewart McAllister

Dai Vaughan is currently engaged in research for a book on Stewart McAllister.

We peer through a doorway to where a man sits hunched over a bench tinkering with something or other. There is a touch of fairytale or of folklore in the bespectacled glance he casts up at our intrusion, elfin and tetchy, wizened yet ageless: of a magical watchmaker surprised at his craft . . . What I describe — from memory, and no doubt inaccurately — is a photograph, taken late in his short life, of Stewart McAllister, editor of **London Can Take It**, **Heart of Britain**, **Words for Battle**, **Listen to Britain**, **Fires Were Started**, **The Silent Village**, **The Eighty Days**, **A Family Portrait**, probably also **Spare Time** and possibly **S.S. Ionian**.

> *You couldn't exactly call him Humphrey's shadow. He had too much substance of his own for that.*
> — A former assistant editor

Many of Humphrey Jennings's admirers employ, tacitly, an argument which goes roughly as follows: Jennings was a very individual film-maker, in the sense that his films manifest continuities of theme and iconography some of which may be traced also in his poems and paintings; therefore his best films must be the most individual, the most personal. While the premiss of this is demonstrably true, the conclusion not only does not follow but requires the disregarding of Jennings's own testimony: for we must assume him to have been responsible for the credit of **Listen to Britain** — arguably his best film, and widely so regarded — which reads, 'Directed and edited by Humphrey Jennings and Stewart McAllister'. It explicitly asserts that this film was not his most individual but his most collaborative.

What sort of person was his collaborator? McAllister was seven years younger than Jennings, having been born in December 1914 in Wishaw, Lanarkshire. From 1931 to 1936 he attended Glasgow School of Art where, although showing considerable promise as a painter, he became increasingly interested in film-making — at that time not an academically reputable activity — and was a party to the first experiments in direct animation than being conducted by his fellow-student, Norman McLaren. His fine arts education co-existed with an interest in science and technology which evidently, in his later years as associate producer with the British Transport Film Unit, equipped him well for his dealings with design engineers in the scripting of films on such subjects as electrification and modernisation of the railways. Despite the commercial and critical successes of **Fires Were Started**, Harry Watt's *Target for Tonight* and David MacDonald's undeservedly forgotten *Men of the Lightship*, McAllister was never tempted by the glamour and financial lures of the features industry, but chose to remain in the field of nationally sponsored documentary from 1937, when he began work with the GPO Unit, until his death in 1962. Characteristically, he left behind him a number of uncompleted electronic devices and two volumes of original engravings by Blake.

It is clear from this outline how closely in some respects the preoccupations of McAllister mirror those of Jennings. The surrealism, of course, is absent; and the social concerns are present not overtly but in the commitment to documentary, which by all accounts was fierce. The parallel may nevertheless be close enough to trouble those commentators whose practice is to invoke an artist's background, ostensibly in explication of the work but in fact as an adjunct to it, so that the work may thereby be assimilated to the artist's persona. Which artist, if not both?

The contributions of editor and director to a film are not easily distinguished. To say that the one assembles material whose shooting the other has overseen does little justice to the intimacy with which two minds may associate to a common purpose. To the extent that such purpose is by custom accredited to the director, we may visualise two people standing, one in front of the other, so that all we see of the further one is that margin which is not shadowed by the nearer. Acquaintance with those films on which Jennings and McAllister worked apart enables us to arrive, after a while, at an intuitive sense of the latter's creative personality as consisting in a certain way of connecting images: a linkage, relying upon a delicate balance between the compositional and the conceptual, wherein each image may assume a symbolic quality, but of a transitory symbolism, limited to context and in no way antagonistic to the shot's status as witness to the vanished moment. Such a mode of cinematic thinking offered the ideal articulation for Jennings's heightened visual vocabulary: offered, indeed, the means for its elevation to the surreal. Despite frequent quarrels — of a legendary passion and brevity, and proof enough of the equality of their dedication — the two worked together whenever they could; and the films which Jennings made without McAllister, however striking in conception or felicitous in local detail, seem to lack a crucial integrative element, as if he had composed them with only one hemisphere of his brain.

Film benefits little from the solitary creativity wished by Romanticism upon the painter and the poet. It is entirely to Jennings's credit that he was able to recognise this; and it is entirely to the discredit of his admirers that they are not. If the point were merely one of parochial dispute within the movie business, there would be no purpose in insisting upon it here. But the undervaluing of technicians' contributions in film-making is part of a broader and deeply political prejudice which, by counterposing only the figure of the isolated individual against the anonymities of mass society, confirms society in its assurance that creative collaboration between equals is a chimera. To approach Jennings through a study of the work of McAllister is to meet him afresh: not as the divinity behind a body of films whose appearance in the world is miraculous, but as a man bringing his considerable talents into harness with those of other people, sometimes succeeding and sometimes failing, engaging with the problems of a specific historical period and answering its demand from within the social and aesthetic perspectives of a movement, and a Unit, of which his own particularity supplied one vital component. That people should present his films as 'personal', in the belief that they are praising them, is especially ironic: for what these films celebrate is sometimes the small working group, sometimes the community and sometimes the nation at large, but never the egregious individual.

It was after Jennings's death in 1950 that McAllister allowed himself to be persuaded to take on the job of producer: but everyone who knew him says that his heart remained in the cutting room; and everyone seems to agree that, for all his efforts in this new capacity, he never really 'found himself' again. It would be picturesque to describe him, in these final years, as the desolate survivor of twins. But that would be an oversimplification. Many things had changed in the pattern of government sponsorship since the days of **London Can Take It**, when by a fluke of providence documentary had attained, with its language newly forged, to a unique position of public trust. Genius, after all, is not the whole story. Had documentary at the outbreak of war been much older and consolidated, or much younger and unprepared, then its great achievements, including those of Jennings and McAllister, would not have been possible.

McAllister's influence persists in a curious form, extending well beyond the circle of those who have heard of him, enshrined in a stock of procedures, habits of mind passed from editor to assistant, a mode of approach to the work. In the Presbyterian church at Wishaw he is commemorated by a stained glass window which bears, over an eagle rising from a thicket of spears, the inscription, 'I will not cease from mental fight.' It is, of course, a quotation from Blake's *Jerusalem*. It is also a quotation from **Words for Battle**.

David Mellor:

Sketch for an Historical Portrait of Humphrey Jennings

Introduction

The work and career of Humphrey Jennings represent a formidable challenge to the as yet unwritten history of modernism in Britain. Known to the general public mainly as a documentary film-maker, Jennings was an artist in many other fields as well, both before and after the watershed of the Second World War. He was a painter (and theorist of modern painting), an experimental photographer, a poet, and intellectual historian, and one of the founders of Mass Observation. Perhaps most importantly of all, he was a practitioner of what has since come to be called intertextuality, reworking and transforming the same material — often beginning with an *objet trouvé* — through various forms and media. Although his diverse career might suggest dilettantism, it was in fact extraordinarily coherent, with each artistic practice in which he was engaged reinforcing and playing off the others. But this coherence was not without its contradictions — contradictions inherent in any modernist project in Britain in the 1930s and 1940s. These contradictions were a condition of Jennings's extraordinary productivity as an experimenter, tirelessly finding paths through the morass of contemporary British culture, and of his subsequent eclipse. His work is now hardly known in any detail, or is known only outside the context that made it so productive. This essay aims to restore and reconstruct some of the context of that work and in particular the relation of his work to modernism in Britain. Just as Jennings audaciously constructed a set of scenographic and poetic variations to reconstellate British culture, so the received map of British modernism (particularly in the region of painting) must be reconstructed to reinsert Jennings's forceful efforts within that period. Within the confines of this introductory essay I can only hope to sketch the outlines of such a project, hoping thereby however to prepare the ground for a full account of Jennings's differential specificity within British modernism.

     I shall examine, necessarily schematically, six moments in Jennings's development, overlapping with the biographical chronology provided by Mary-Lou Jennings to accompany the documentation about his career elsewhere in this book. My schema begins (1.) with his position up to 1930, and follows (2.) his transformation through his encounter with pictorial modernism between 1930 and 1933, (3.) his change of status and recruitment into documentary film-making in 1934, (4.) the complex moment around Mass Observation, (5.) his filmic *Gesamtkunstwerke* of the Second World War, and finally (6.) his return to the primacy of painting and to pre- and post-industrial landscapes in the late 1940s. It is also hoped that this chronological succession will not mask the traces of the interaction and continuity of many authorial drives and motifs latent in what I shall call the Jennings-text: that group of paintings, films, poems and photographs spanning the period from 1930 to 1950.

63

The House in the Woods / [1937]
Tate Gallery, London

1. From Antiquarianism to the Signifier as Content

A constant determination in the Jennings-text was his particular notion of inter-media linkages and polysemy. In this critical perception he was shaped by the innovative teaching of English literature at Cambridge by I.A.Richards and by the patrimony of that eclectic synaesthesia found in the Arts and Crafts movement in which both his parents were lodged. The allusions of emblems, decorative symbols and devices, and of scholarly reflexiveness over style and motif in drama and poetry, were all well imprinted on Jennings by the end of the 1920s. That endless ambiguous play of signifiers within a poem or painting that would so characterise his later work was first seeded within a framework of antiquarianism and concern with incunabula. It was within this structure that he found the Fitzwilliam Museum in Cambridge with its gigantic assemblage of paintings and objects so suggestive — he symptomatically described it as a 'glorious mix-up'. This is revealing: for he perceived a transcendent ('glorious') cultural assemblage which acted like an irritant on his critical antiquarianism, constantly juxtaposing different historical modes. Jennings the *bricoleur* of the 1930s and 1940s can here be seen in formation, while he shared in Richards's and his fellow-student William Empson's rediscovery of rhetorical, literary and dramatic devices — pastorals, triumphs and elegies. He began too his meditation on the historical roles of poets who had practised these forms — the private rentier poet such as Thomas Gray (his doctoral subject), or the state panegyrist or martial laureate. He visited Rome in 1928 and, as the decade closed, made contact with the international neo-classicism of the period. It was a saturating style which, via Bloomsbury, had its outpost in Cambridge. Jennings collaborated with Lydia Lopokova, wife of John Maynard Keynes, on a production of Stravinsky's *The Soldier's Tale*, and came under the influence of the painting of Duncan Grant, which had been hailed in the 1920s by Roger Fry for its 'Elizabethan' wittiness and had already encompassed Picasso's neo-classicism. Grant's style was manipulated by Jennings for two ends: scenographically, in his stage designs and paintings of Harlequins (stock items of neo-classicism), and for lyrical landscape paintings of Suffolk and Essex barns and fields. He began to engage actively with the problems of style-conscious reflexiveness, remaking Gainsborough and Constable motifs according to the codes of Matisse and Grant.

But it was theatrical scenography that mainly preoccupied him as a painter: he was a scene designer for pageants and operas, which provided the site for his first inter-media experiment. Meanwhile his reflexiveness over style led him to a point, about 1930, when the scenic backdrops and props, and their signifying codes, became objects for his smaller private paintings. Pictorial play with different scenery painting techniques and their artifice had marginally interested Sickert in his spatial experiments with point of view in his theatre paintings, but to configure a painting exclusively around the discourses of scenography was something novel; it was a kind of meta-painting which had, perhaps, its nearest point of reference in contemporary paintings by Ben Nicholson. Nicholson's paintings also dealt with signifiers as content, though in his case the signifiers were drawn from the source of Parisian *natures-mortes* — a genre which, twenty years later, Jennings was to interrogate and deconstruct as part of an attempt to Anglicise modernist iconography.

Photograph with portrait of Byron / MLJ

2. Modernism and the Re-Representation of History

Already familiar with the Parisian avant-garde through the arts and letters magazines *Transition* and *Cahiers d'Art*, Jennings had first-hand contact with modernism in Paris when he attempted to live there, intermittently, in 1930 and 1931. His stays radically recast his sensibility into Surrealist categories. He wrote from Paris in September 1931. 'I already feel utterly different about painting, more concentrated and excited and more myself . . . as I used to feel about scenery'. In Surrealism and post-Cubist painting generally he found an alternative to the arcane codes of neo-classicism. He hoped, ideologically, that a modernist system of proportions, a new spatial system and refurbished iconography would restore a 'Rubens-like heroism'. That cultural criterion of the heroic became a significant goal for Jennings, but revealed a contradiction. As an unreconstructed antiquarian he accepted the patriarchal authority of classical origins, refusing to relinquish them and indeed affirming them in his 1936 critique of the weaknesses inherent in British Surrealism. On the other hand his writings on art in 1931 swept aside the preceding, first generation of modernism, proclaiming Cubism already dead for six years. Justifying this moment of break, he wrote, 'Freedom had to be regained', an aim he envisaged being implemented by the 'jeune peinture', with Masson, Borès, Cossio, Roux and Miró prominent in their ranks.

In the place of the monochrome, formal, rectilinear and wedge-like compositions of Cubism, the new space initiated by Miró was polychrome, fluid, ambiguous: it gave directly on to fantasy projections and the multiple play of signifiers. It was perhaps Miró who wrought the most drastic shift in Jennings's pictorial codes. Miró's *Circus Horse* series of 1926-27 did not just happen to refer to one of Jennings's preferred icons, the horse, but resanctioned the representation of personal mythologies, a zone excluded from Cubism. Jennings, in his photographs of the late 1930s, attempted various anamorphic and collage reworkings of his own horse paintings. But Miró's major contribution to the Jennings-text was to provide an open licence for visual pastiche and transcription, an opportunity to re-represent historical images again, now figured by modernist pictorial codes. In his *Imaginary Portraits* of 1929 Miró had treated paintings by Raphael and by 17th-century Dutch masters and a Georgian portrait of 1750 as signifiers to be modernised. This provided Jennings with a rationale for painting Guy Fawkes, Karl Marx, Charles Darwin and William Morris — historically resonant British or adopted British personages — in a mode that surpassed the previous code for such representations, prising them from the tonal, *juste-milieu*, academic, naturalistic style that had been stabilised since the end of the 19th century. In its place Jennings introduced the polychrome, fluid constructs of Miró, Dali and Masson. His pronounced antiquarianism and modernism could, by 1932, be yoked together. Surrealism had now repopulated painting and legislated myth as viable content. The corollary of his discovery of Surrealism and its methods of dream transcription and automatism was, of course, a comprehensive reading of Freud, which he seems to have undertaken from 1932 and was still engaged on in 1938.

65

['The Sower'] / (1933) / JD14

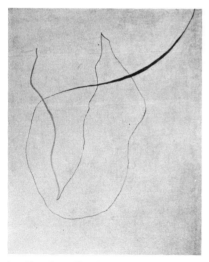

Joan Miró: *Circus Horse* / (1927)
Coll. G.Duthuit

3. Documentary Film as the 'Magnificent System'

Up to 1934 Jennings had been attempting, unsuccessfully, to establish himself as an artist — an Edwardian rebel artist, he fantasised, like Galsworthy's Jolyon — and working on his doctorate. As one of the editors, along with Empson and Bronowski, of the magazine *Experiment*, Jennings had reproduced two abstract paintings by a young French artist who was studying English literature at Cambridge in 1929, Henri Cartier-Bresson. In contrast, by 1934, Cartier-Bresson had become one of the leading exponents of candid realist reportage, using a Leica still camera loaded with adapted film stock. A new realism, supported, strengthened and broadened by the new photo-mechanical technologies, was to become, along with Surrealism, one of the leading issues on the modernist agenda by the mid-1930s. Defections and transits across the pictorial media, from painting into photography and film, became a conspicuous feature of the cultural map. These tendencies were intensified by the Depression, which, among its other effects, all but destroyed the market for modernist painting. There were therefore distinct economic reasons which drove painters (like William Coldstream) into the GPO Film Unit and other governmental or commercial agencies. It was the proffered shelter of a regular wage that finally induced Jennings to join a profession that he had expressly rejected a few years earlier. 'I should hate doing films really . . . simply I want to draw,' he had written in a letter to his wife Cicely in 1929.

One of his first working contacts at the GPO Film Unit — his apprenticeship, in fact — was with Alberto Cavalcanti, who had an extensive background in Parisian Surrealism. Indeed, as it was mediated to many British artists, Surrealism appeared to be pre-eminently a film form. Bunuel's *Un Chien andalou* and *L'Age d'or* had a determining impact on the British documentarist photographer Bill Brandt, for example. Jennings's transition and change of status was not unusual, but it was to effect a marked displacement in his work, in the Jennings-text. For around 1934-36 corporate mega-visual forms, especially documentary — representations for the newly emerging corporate agencies such as the GPO, Shell, BP, Milk Marketing Board, London Transport, etc — appeared to be increasingly occupying a new central ground in pictorial practice, marginalising the more traditional manual art media and their private functions. In effect, and paradoxically, his new role returned him to his earlier, scholarly concerns with the classical rhetorics of public address and spectacle — the triumph and elegy — but now inflected within a populist frame. His absorption into the GPO affected the non-visual areas of his production. It was from the same date, 1934, that he also began to extend Imagist poetic forms, familiar from childhood reading of his parents' copies of *The New Age*, through the adoption of journalistic-documentarist-reportage models. The new experimental formats of 'Reports' and 'Popular Narratives' depended on objectified word-collages, very often modified Surrealist narratives enunciated through the persona of a mock 18th-century mandarin or encyclopaedist, an inventor of History as well as its recorder.

The dominance of 'camera reality', of the *sachlich* record as a possible object of fantasy, was now paramount in the Jennings-text. Camera reality, he had come to believe, had utterly outstripped and marginalised certain established poetic roles and postures. For future Coronations, he wrote, the poet laureate might only make shift by 'making an analysis of [the] emotion [of] the camera photographs' of the procession and ceremony. Meanwhile the structure of pictorial production which he entered had developed its own, pre-existing type of filmic lyrical pastoral — as for example in one of the first GPO films he saw on induction in 1934, Evelyn Spice's *Spring on the Farm*. Within the Jennings-text a self-definition of his new methods was forming. It lay at the intersection of his consciousness of the photo-mechanical nature of the mass media, of the still operative Surrealist categories of the *objet trouvé* and the ready-made (the Duchampian object of labour and use transformed into object of art display), and of the cinematic technique of cutting and montage (which may have represented for Jennings the final hypertrophy of Cubism). Combined with his perpetual allegiance to the activity of English literary criticism, these concepts produced an obsessive image, a mock-archaic and trans-cendental object — a Benjaminesque notion of Documentary as the 'magnificent system'. He elaborated this in his poem, or 'Report', *The Boyhood of Byron*: 'The labours of the antiquary, the verbal critic, the collator of mouldering manuscripts, may be preparing the way for the achievements of some splendid genius, who may combine their minute details into some magnificent system, or evolve from a multitude of particulars some general principle, destined to illuminate the career of future ages'.

4. Towards the Poet-Reporter and Mass Observation

Aside from the evocation in *The Boyhood of Byron* of the projective camera obscura, prototype of the camera, the image of illumination, and more importantly the illuminator, plays a central part in the Jennings-text from 1934 onwards. It is an image which has 18th-century connotations, rooted in the reforming intellectual elite of the Enlightenment. Such a role, in Britain in the 1930s and 1940s, was coveted by Grierson and many of the documentarists. 'Is it possible,' one of them wrote, 'that the business of national education is passing, by default, from the offices of Whitehall to the Public Relations departments of the great corporations?'

In the Jennings-text from the late 1930s, light discloses truth, or is decomposed and, in splitting or in recomposition through a prism, reveals colour. There recurs a symbolic opposition between greyness (associated with funereality and the industrial landscape) and colour as a productive force. In his poem *As the Sun*, the patriarchal incarnation of the sun places a prohibition on the sight of colour. Nature, in *As the Sun* and in *Peacock Coal*, suffers neutralisation, a repression of colour, which, in the latter poem, is enforced by the patriarchs of the Industrial Revolution itself. This proces is then in turn negated by industrial labour. In Jennings's system of symbolic substitutions, colour is eventually recovered from the industrial masses during war time and under the Attlee government: communalism and populism act as the new organisational prisms that release the 'prismatic radiance of humanity' in a painting like *Canteen* (1944), a polychrome reworking of a scene from **Listen to Britain** further reworked in 1949.

In 1936 the symbolic order of British society was on the verge of breaking up, or so it seemed to Jennings, in his meditations on the deathliness

Listen to Britain: Flanagan and Allen

Painting / [c.1949: from a photograph probably of the Flanagan and Allen audience] / JD102

Drawing / [c.1949: see above] / JD86

inherent in the 'ghostly' black and white film of George V's funeral. It seemed so, too, to other journalists who came together to form the Mass Observation organisation. The year began with the passing of George V, the national patriarch, and continued with the removal through abdication of another monarch, Edward VIII, and the substitution of a third, George VI. A great national monument, the Crystal Palace, was destroyed by fire in the same year. In Europe this was the year of the Popular Front in France, but also of Franco's assault, backed by Germany and Italy, against the Spanish Republic. But it was with strictly national portents and omens that Tom Harrisson and Charles Madge were concerned when they joined with Jennings at the beginning of 1937 to found Mass Observation, inviting, through the columns of the *Daily Mirror* and *New Statesman*, mass participation in a project to describe everyday life in Britain. By co-ordinating the results of questionnaires about recollected dreams, habits, prejudices, wishes and daydreams, the leaders of Mass Observation hoped — clearly on a Freudian model — to examine a collective discourse and to analyse and diagnose a society whose channels of communication seemed pathologically blocked.

Jennings's only major publication was constructed out of his arrangement of Mass Observation responses to inquiries into private and public behaviour during the coronation of George VI on 12 May 1937. In his report on his own behaviour that day (he photographed crowds watching the Coronation in the Mall, not far from where — as it happened — Cartier-Bresson was also photographing) he revealed his fascination with the paraphernalia of the newest of all the mass media — television, fully deployed for the first time for that event. With his collage/reportage documentary book, *May 12th*, Jennings's 'magnificent system' became a gigantic concordance of texts held in place by the realist-documentarist device of one (special-yet-ordinary) day's time elapsing — a favourite rhetorical form of photo-magazine reportage in the 1930s and 1940s, and previously pioneered in film by Cavalcanti, Ruttmann and Vertov. The synchronous texts were sifted by Jennings as solicited testimonies that might reveal the latent significations of a British unconsciousness, an endless palimpsest written on and over by many but co-ordinated by one. Pursuing this vein of democratic Surrealism (somewhat in the mode of the early, quasi-bureaucratic *Surréaliste Centrale*) Jennings wrote on the mass psychology of the snapshot in terms that, more precisely, recall the independent but parallel notion in Walter Benjamin of an optical, photographic unconsciousness. Jennings also practised a self-analysis of his own 'art' discourse, mapping the associations that he could trace in his work between a multiplicity of displacements of ideas and images, both pictorial and scriptural. The resulting 'map' (reproduced on p.20), in conjunction with his paintings and a poem of the same date entitled *The Origin of Colour*, offers a part-key to the state of the Jennings-text as of 1938.

Despite a public admonition by Paul Nougé against the use of Freud's own reductionist forays into sociology, Jennings's interest in the social applications of certain Freudian extensions of Surrealism (such as attempting to read off a kind of urban unconsciousness from news headlines, advertisements and shop windows) intensified after his intimacy with Breton, Eluard and Duchamp in 1936-38. Along with Breton and Roland Penrose he organised the International Surrealist Exhibition in London in June 1936. One of his contributions was a collage-satire of Kitchener, the venerated military leader of the Great War, represented by Jennings as a minotaur — a contribution which provoked a minor news scandal in the conservative *Daily Mail*.

One guise which reconciled the twin demands of the Surrealist and the Documentarist was that of the Poet-Reporter. In his BBC broadcasts in 1938 on the general theme of 'Poetry and the Public', Jennings posited a unity which had once existed in English Literature, before the advent of the mass media, in which 'the poet was a kind of reporter'; and 'poet-reporter' was in fact the title adopted by Charles Madge during these years, echoing the utopian hopes of Mass Observation to have reconciled science and art after their separation brought about by the Industrial Revolution. It was also Madge, then a Marxist-Leninist, who provided Jennings with the 'text' for one of his fullest and most significant photographs, *Daily Worker* (1937), by discussing with him Lenin's theory of human labour inscribed into the production of a manufactured object like a table. Like much of the Jennings-text, this photograph is concerned with the re-representation of an historical fragment — in this case a copy of the Communist newspaper represented as a derelicted discarded emblem whose positioning in the picture undercuts the optimism of the triumphal headline and portrait.

Although he kept his distance from the Communist orthodoxies of the late 1930s, the reform programme of the Popular Front government in France did interest him, particularly its introduction of paid holidays and a shorter working week. (He was briefly in Paris in 1937 to visit the Exposition in company with his patron Peggy Guggenheim, and it was on this occasion that he also first made the acquaintance of Duchamp.) Patterns of working-class leisure were a central concern of Mass Observation. The documentarist photographer Humphrey Spender, who, like Charles Madge, worked as a reporter for the *Daily Mirror*, recorded the Wakes Week in Blackpool for Mass Observation in 1937. Jennings took up this theme in his film **Spare Time** (1939), which was partly set in Bolton (where Tom Harrisson was based). In this film leisure is represented as a narrow time-corridor of gratification in industrial society 'as things now stand'. Pigeon-fancying, darts and football are presided over by a statue of Richard Cobden, the personification of liberal capitalist ideology. This pictorial motif of the presence of industry and patriarchy embodied as a statue Jennings had derived from the proto-surrealist iconography of Giorgio De Chirico, a potent influence also on Bill Brandt's contemporary documentary photographs of northern industrial towns.

Another scandal was precipitated by the film among Jennings's colleagues in the documentary movement by its depiction of the signs of a mass popular culture in a *sachlich*, unpicturesque manner. Prior to the conscious elaboration of Pop Art by the Independent Group at the ICA in the mid-1950s, **Spare Time** offered perhaps the strongest concentration of pop iconography in any work by a British artist — comic books, pop songs, football-pool advertisements. Alongside its candid, Spenderesque view of the factuality of industrial leisure, the crucial novelty about the film was the way it revolved about the exploration of the

'Daily Worker' / [1937] / JD62

Statue of Richard Cobden (formerly in Peel Park, Salford), from **Spare Time**

signifiers of pop culture, areas that would provide the site for the work of the pop painters of the 1950s and early 1960s in London, while in other respects it looks forward even further to the intertextual pictorial projects of R.B.Kitaj in the 1960s and 1970s.

5. Orchestration and Scenography of the National Patriotic War

One of the features of the Jennings-text during the Second World War is the heightened tension between the signifiers of high and pop mass culture, especially through the coding of music on his film soundtracks. This extended the juxta-position of baroque music and dance-band and kazoo music already present in **Spare Time**. Music becomes the dominant organising category of the films and poems, the matrix through which the signifying elements of Britain at War became, as he noted in a written outline for **Listen to Britain**, 'all one symphony'. His assemblage format, the 'magnificent system', was shifting towards a kind of synaesthesia, a kind of filmic *Gesamtkunstwerk*, a documentarist-baroque in which the rhetorical modes of Pageants, Triumphs and Masques could be remobilised under the ideological aegis of the Churchillian renaissance. The poets had, he wrote, once more learned to be patriotic. So had film-makers, as the presence of the Pageant or Triumph in contemporary films by Powell and Pressburger bears witness.

The crisis of ideological institutions at the end of the 1930s — the crisis that had brought Mass Observation into existence — was halted abruptly with the fall of France and a new symbolic order emerged. The new ideological configuration is signified and reproduced in the chaotic assemblage of aristocratic paraphernalia mixed with functional populist ónes in the pageant of Dressing Station 76 in **Listen to Britain** (1942), where a baroque statue of Charles I mingles with the steel helmets of the ambulance crews.

The paternal, communitarian systems of the Commonwealth Party, as much as those of Beveridge or even Churchill, fell back on the rhetoric and discourse of a moralising, classicising English Literature. Jennings's scholarly enquiries ten years earlier into the role of the martial laureates could now be enacted. The split role of the poet reporter was discarded for the return of the martial laureate; the sense of the Heroic Renaissance that he had sought in post-Cubist art, with its additive, free space and revived mythologies, was transposed in his 1943-44 poem *I Saw Harlequin*, which juxtaposes the dance of Harlequin to the advance of the Red Army on the eastern front. (Accompanying British Commandos on the first assault wave on Sicily in 1943, Jennings wrote of them in terms of artist-warriors.) The cultural plurality of the wartime totality was summed up by Jennings as the paradox of the recombined nation: 'When everybody is in uniform, nobody is; just as punishment creates crime, so also restriction creates freedom'. The lyrical natural landscape of the Jennings-text of the 1930s, neutralised through the deformation of the Industrial revolution, became in the 1940s a signifier of renewed plenitude, absorbing into itself the martial emblems of fighter aircraft and ack-ack guns amongst skyscapes and trees. In one (unrealised) film treatment, Spitfires and

Listen to Britain / Dressing Station 76

Hurricanes became thoroughly naturalised as part of landscape, with a Suffolk farmworker suggesting, in a monologue, that the warplanes no longer disturbed bird life in the countryside — indeed they looked like partridges.

6. From the 'Invention of History' to the 'Amenity of Landscape'

In the post-war years the Jennings-text, far from losing impetus, being beset by anxiety or losing direction (as is sometimes alleged), is constructed by a new series of meanings. The recombination through the wartime patriarch is followed by the new order installed by the 1945-50 Labour government. In **The Cumberland Story** (1947) productive effort and labour are redeemed within a Utopian Socialist perspective. In an untitled poem written in 1947-48 Jennings viewed the industrial vista, concentrating on the labour that had produced it, and celebrated the possibility that the complex of building and production could be matched by the signifying marks and gestures of painting. The signifiers of labour are dissolved back into the townscape:

Not one of the things done
Not one man whose cunning produced the littlest piece of what I see in the whole
But is represented by some stroke of brush, flake of snow, speck of soot
In a picture of how many million touches.

Beginning in the 1930s and carrying on through the 1940s Jennings had collected and collaged together texts on the development of the Industrial Revolution and its impact on the 'mentalities' of the 18th and 19th centuries, all for an uncompleted mega-text, like *May 12th*, to have been titled *Pandaemonium* — its name indicating its many-layered palimpsest of voices. But as the 1940s progressed, Jennings — who had never associated himself with the ideologies of triumphant managerial technocracy which flourished both before and after the war — came more and more to assert the values of a post-industrial symbolic order of Utopian Socialism. His models were Robert Owen, William Cobbett and William Morris. A poem of 1941 contrasts present-day Lanark with the Utopian community of New Lanark founded by Owen in the early 19th century, while in 1947 Jennings describes his politics as 'those of William Cobbett'. He painted 'Imaginary Portraits' of Morris, whose image also appears in his last film, **Family Portrait.** In this, the era of the New Towns movement, it could easily have seemed to him that many of the ideas of the Arts and Crafts movement with which he had grown up, were coming to fulfilment. He also visited pre-industrial Burma shortly after the war, recording its ceremonies and customs for a film treatment, and his observation of the still colonial East makes a striking contrast with the contemporary reportage of Cartier-Bresson in South-East Asia and Nationalist China just before its collapse.

Pastoral was still the operative category, however, and through much of the late 1940s his effort was redirected towards painted versions inside this genre. Post-Cubist modernist landscape had also been the site of pictorial work by Graham

Burmese photograph / [1947] / MLJ

Photograph of ox and plough,
from Jennings's papers

72

Sutherland and Paul Nash in the 1930s and 1940s. They had endeavoured to disclose a specifically national *Heimat*, a British counterpart to the painted locations of international modernism — the South of France for example. This procedure of substituting national cultural signifiers for foreign or cosmopolitan ones was present in the Jennings-text of the late 1940s. In his paintings and poems of the time, the c plough, and more particularly its shadow, bears the symbolic capacity to match and replace the guitar in the iconography of modernism. There may have been residual traces of Jennings's fascination with Duchamp's machinism in his elevation of the plough to iconic status, particularly given the key role that shadows of objects play in Duchamp's aesthetic. In his poem *La Charrue* (The Plough), which he may have addressed directly to Eluard or Breton, Jennings insists that 'the plough is the English guitar'. In another variant of the poem, his attempted system of national iconographic displacement is more explicit:

> For the guitar's plane, the plough
> In the plate's place, the wheel
> In the wine's wheat . . .

And he carries on, cancelling out the signifiers of Parisian modernist *nature morte* (wallpaper, tablecloth, bottles etc.) with more signifiers, like windmills, drawn from the repertory of the (British) landscape. 'So to assemble the still life and the Suffolk scene.'

Horse and plough / [c.1948]

Filmography

1934:

Post Haste
GPO Film Unit
Producer: John Grierson
Director: Humphrey Jennings
Length: 10 minutes

Pett and Pott
GPO Film Unit
Producer: John Grierson
Director/Script/Writer/Editor:
   A.Cavalcanti
Associate Directors:
   Basil Wright, Stuart Legg
Sets: Humphrey Jennings
Sound recording: John Cox
Music: Walter Leigh
Length: 33 minutes

Locomotives
GPO Film Unit
Director: Humphrey Jennings
Musical Direction: John Foulds
Music: Schubert, arr. Foulds
Length: 10 minutes

The Story of the Wheel
GPO Film Unit
Editor: Humphrey Jennings
Length: 12 minutes

1936:

The Birth of the Robot
Shell-Mex BP
Gasparcolor
Producer/director: Len Lye
Script: C.H.David
Photography: Alex Strasser
Colour decor and production:
   Humphrey Jennings
Models: John Banting,
   Alan Fanner
Sound recording: Jack Ellit
Music: Gustav Holst
Length: 7 minutes

1938:

Penny Journey
GPO Film Unit
Director: Humphrey Jennings
Photography: H.E.(Chick) Fowle,
   W.B.Pollard
Length: 8 minutes

Design for Spring
Distributor: ABFD
Dufaycolor
Director: Humphrey Jennings
Length: 20 minutes
Made with the dress designer
   Norman Hartnell

Speaking from America
GPO Film Unit
Producer: A.Cavalcanti
Director: Humphrey Jennings
Photography: W.B.Pollard,
   Fred Gamage
Commentator: Robin Duff
Diagrams: J.Chambers
Sound: Ken Cameron
Length: 10 minutes

1939:

Spare Time
(Working title: *British Workers*)
GPO Film Unit
Producer: A.Cavalcanti
Director/Scriptwriter:
   Humphrey Jennings
Assistant Director: D.V.Knight
Photography: Chick Fowle
Commentator: Laurie Lee
Sound: Yorke Scarlett
Music: Steel, Peach and Tozer
   Phoenix Works Band,
   Manchester Victorians'
   Carnival Band,
   Handel Male Voice Choir
Length: 18 minutes

The First Days
(Alternative title:
A City Prepares)
GPO Film Unit/ABPC
Producer: A.Cavalcanti
Directors: Humphrey Jennings,
   Harry Watt, Pat Jackson
Editor: R.Q.McNaughton
Commentary: Robert Sinclair
Length: 23 minutes

English Harvest
Dufaycolor
Director: Humphrey Jennings
Length: 9 minutes

S.S.Ionian
(Alternative Title: *Her Last Trip*)
GPO Film Unit
Director: Humphrey Jennings
Length: 20 minutes

1940:

Spring Offensive
(Alternative title:
An Unrecorded Victory)
GPO Film Unit
Producer: A.Cavalcanti
Director: Humphrey Jennings
Photography: Chick Fowle, Eric Cross
Script: Hugh Gray
Writer of commentary: A.G.Street
Designer: Edward Carrick
Editor: Geoff Foot
Sound: Ken Cameron
Length: 20 minutes

Welfare of the Workers
GPO Film Unit for
   the Ministry of Information
Producer: Harry Watt
Director: Humphrey Jennings
Photography: Jonah Jones
Editor: Jack Lee
Sound: Ken Cameron
Commentary: Ritchie Calder
Length: 10 minutes

London Can Take It
(Alternative title of shorter film
for domestic distribution:
Britain Can Take It)
GPO Film Unit for
   Ministry of Information
Directors: Humphrey Jennings/
   Harry Watt
Photography: Jonah Jones,
   Chick Fowle
Commentary: Quentin Reynolds
Length: 10 minutes

1941:

Heart of Britain
(Alternative title of
slightly longer export version:
This is England
Eire title: *Undaunted*)
Production: Ian Dalrymple for
    Ministry of Information
Director: Humphrey Jennings
Photography: Chick Fowle
Editor: Stewart McAllister
Sound: Ken Cameron
Commentary: Jack Holmes
Length: 9 minutes

Words for Battle
Production: Ian Dalrymple for
    Crown Film Unit
Director: Humphrey Jennings
Editor: Stewart McAllister
Sound: Ken Cameron
Commentary spoken by:
    Laurence Olivier
Length: 8 minutes

1942:

Listen to Britain
Production: Ian Dalrymple for
    Crown Film Unit
Directed and Edited:
    Humphrey Jennings/
    Stewart McAllister
Photography: Chick Fowle
Sound: Ken Cameron
Length: 20 minutes

1943:

Fires Were Started
(Alternative Title: *I Was a Fireman*)
Production: Ian Dalrymple for
    Crown Film Unit
Director/Script:
    Humphrey Jennings
Photography:
    C.Pennington-Richards
Editor: Stewart McAllister
Story collaboration:
    Maurice Richardson
Music: William Alwyn
Length: 80 minutes

The Silent Village
Production: Humphrey Jennings for
    Crown Film Unit
Director/Script:
    Humphrey Jennings
Photography: Chick Fowle
Editor: Stewart McAllister
Sound: Jock May
Length: 36 minutes

1944:

The True Story of Lili Marlene
Production: J.B.Holmes for
    Crown Film Unit
Director/Script:
    Humphrey Jennings
Photography: Chick Fowle
Editor: Sid Stone
Music: Denis Blood
Length: 30 minutes

The 80 Days
Production: Humphrey Jennings for
    Crown Film Unit
Director: Humphrey Jennings
Commentary: Ed Murrow
Length: 14 minutes

V1
(Made wholly for overseas use
with same material as *The 80 Days*
but re-edited and with a new
commentary)
Production: Humphrey Jennings for
    Crown Film Unit
Commentary: Fletcher Markle
Length: 10 minutes

1944-45:

A Diary for Timothy
(Released 1946)
Production: Basil Wright for
    Crown Film Unit
Director/Script:
    Humphrey Jennings
Photography: Fred Gamage
Editors: Alan Osbiston, Jenny Hutt
Sound: Ken Cameron, Jock May
Music: Richard Addinsell
Commentary: E.M.Forster
Spoken by: Michael Redgrave
Length: 38 minutes

1945:

A Defeated People
Production: Basil Wright for
    Crown Film Unit
(for Directorate of Army
    Kinematography)
Director/Script:
    Humphrey Jennings
Photography: Army Film Unit
Commentary spoken by
    William Hartnell
Music: Guy Warrack
Length: 19 minutes

1947:

The Cumberland Story
Production: Alexander Shaw for
    Crown Film Unit
(COI for Ministry of Fuel and Power)
Director/Script:
    Humphrey Jennings
Photography: Chick Fowle
Editor: Jocelyn Jackson
Music: Arthur Benjamin
Length: 39 minutes

1949:

Dim Little Island
Production: Wessex Films
for Central Office of Information
Producer/Director:
    Humphrey Jennings
Photography: Martin Curtis
Editor: Bill Megarry
Music: Ralph Vaughan Williams
Commentary: Osbert Lancaster,
    John Ormston, James Fisher,
    Ralph Vaughan Williams
Length: 11 minutes

1950:

Family Portrait
Production: Ian Dalrymple for
    Wessex Films
Director/Script:
    Humphrey Jennings
Photography: Martin Curtis
Editor: Stewart McAllister
Sound: Ken Cameron
Music: John Greenwood
Commentary spoken by:
    Michael Goodliffe
Length: 25 minutes

Bibliography

Published Writings

'The Duke' and 'The Charcoal Burner'. *Two Plays from the Perse School*, W.Heffer and Sons Ltd, Cambridge, 1921.

'Song'. *Public School Verse* Vol.IV 1923-24, edited by Martin Gilkes, Richard Hughes and P.H.B.Lyon, W.Heinemann Ltd.

'Design and the Theatre'. *Experiment* No.1, November 1928, Cambridge.

'Odd Thoughts at the Fitzwilliam'. *Experiment* No.2, February 1929, Cambridge.

'Notes on Marvell's "To His Coy Mistress"'. *Experiment* No.2, February 1929, Cambridge.

'Rock Painting and "La Jeune Peinture"' (with Gerald Noxon). *Experiment* No.7, Spring 1931, Cambridge.

'A Reconsideration of Herrick' (with J.M.Reeves). *Experiment* No.7, Spring 1931, Cambridge.

'The Theatre'. *The Arts Today*, edited by Geoffrey Grigson, Bodley Head, 1935.

'Three Reports'. *Contemporary Poetry and Prose*, edited by Roger Roughton, No.1, June 1936.

'Three Reports'. *Contemporary Poetry and Prose*, edited by Roger Roughton, August/September 1936.

Review of *Surrealism* by Herbert Read. *Contemporary Poetry and Prose*, December 1936.

'The Boyhood of Byron'. *Contemporary Poetry and Prose*, December 1936 (republished in *London Bulletin* No.12, April 1939).

'Report on the Industrial Revolution'. *Contemporary Poetry and Prose*, Spring 1937.

May the Twelfth: Mass Observation Day Surveys 1937. Co-edited with Charles Madge. Faber and Faber, September 1937.

'In Magritte's Paintings'. *London Gallery Bulletin* No.1, April 1938.

'Prose Poem' ['As the Sun']. *London Bulletin* No.2, May 1938.

'The Iron Horse'. *London Bulletin* No.3, June 1938.

Editor, *London Bulletin* No.4, July 1938.

'Who Does That Remind You Of?'. *London Bulletin* No.6, October 1938.

'Two American Poems'. *London Bulletin* No.11, March 1939.

'Notes on the Cleaned Pictures: Colorado Claro'. *Our Time*, December 1947.

Review of *The English* edited by Ernest Barker. *Times Literary Supplement*, 7 August 1948.

'Working Sketches of an Orchestra'. In Hubert Foss and Notel Goodwin, *London Symphony: Portrait of an Orchestra*, The Naldrett Press, London 1954.

Poems. The Weekend Press, New York, 1951.

Broadcasts

'Plagiarism in Poetry'. BBC National Programme, December 1937.

'The Disappearance of Ghosts'. BBC National Programme, February 1938.

'The Modern Poet and the Public'. BBC National Programme, April 1938.

'The Poet and the Public in the Past'. BBC National Programme, May 1938.

'Understanding Modern Poetry'. BBC National Programme, May 1938.

'The Poet Laureateship'. BBC National Programme, June 1938.

'Poetry and National Life'. BBC National Programme, June 1938.

'Science Review No.10' (on James Nasmyth's steam hammer). BBC National Programme, May 1939.

'Pourquoi j'aime la France'. BBC French Service, February 1941.

'The Silent Village'. BBC Home Service, May 1943.

British Library Cataloguing Card Data

Humphrey Jennings.
1. Jennings, Humphrey
2. Moving-picture producers and directors
-Great Britain-Biography
791.43'0233'0924   PN1998.A3J/
ISBN 0-85170-118-3

Published by the British Film Institute
127 Charing Cross Road / London WC2H 0EA
in association with
Riverside Studios
Crisp Road, London W6

ISBN 0 85170 118 3

Printed in England by Wise Printing Ltd, Hayes, Middlesex
Typeset by Padnall Printers Ltd, London